65+
THE BEST YEARS OF YOUR LIFE
With lessons for people of every age

Peter Bowden
University of Sydney

Series in Sociology

Copyright © 2019 Vernon Press, an imprint of Vernon Art and Science Inc, on behalf of the author.

All rights reserved. No part of this publication may be reproduced, stored in a retrieval system, or transmitted in any form or by any means, electronic, mechanical, photocopying, recording, or otherwise, without the prior permission of Vernon Art and Science Inc.

www.vernonpress.com

In the Americas:
Vernon Press
1000 N West Street,
Suite 1200, Wilmington,
Delaware 19801
United States

In the rest of the world:
Vernon Press
C/Sancti Espiritu 17,
Malaga, 29006
Spain

Series in Sociology

Library of Congress Control Number: 2018952656

ISBN: 978-1-62273-450-4

Product and company names mentioned in this work are the trademarks of their respective owners. While every care has been taken in preparing this work, neither the authors nor Vernon Art and Science Inc. may be held responsible for any loss or damage caused or alleged to be caused directly or indirectly by the information contained in it.

Every effort has been made to trace all copyright holders, but if any have been inadvertently overlooked the publisher will be pleased to include any necessary credits in any subsequent reprint or edition.

Table of Contents

LIST OF FIGURES	v
INTRODUCTION	vii
FOREWORD	xi
Chapter 1 **UNHAPPINESS IN OLDER PEOPLE**	1
Chapter 2 **THE EARLY PHILOSOPHERS**	5
Chapter 3 **MARCUS TULLIUS CICERO**	19
Chapter 4 **THE ANATOMY OF MELANCHOLY**	25
Chapter 5 **MILL, RUSSELL AND DARWIN**	31
Chapter 6 **THE MODERN RESEARCHERS**	37
Chapter 7 **THE FINDINGS OF THE SURVEY**	49
Chapter 8 **RELIGION, A HEALTHY LIFE, AND DEATH**	61
Chapter 9 **THE ROLE OF GOVERNMENT**	73
Chapter 10 **BRINGING IT TOGETHER**	83
AFTERWORD	93
REFERENCES	111
INDEX	117

LIST OF FIGURES

1.1 Black Dog Institute	2
1.2 The Geriatric Depression Test	3
2.1 Aristotle's 12 virtues	10
6.1 Character Strengths & Virtues	42
7.1 Questionnaire	50
7.2 Reasons Behind Yes Answers	53
7.3 Reasons Behind No Answers	54
7.4 Average age of YES and NO responders	55
7.5 The Golden Oldies	56
9.1 Australian priorities	76
9.2 Unted Nations. Global Survey of the World's Priorities	76
10.1 The Author's Priorities	90

INTRODUCTION

This is a book about happiness, about what it is, about the responsibilities of individuals and governments to promote happiness. Some studies and media reports suggest that older people are unhappy, prone to depression. Peter Bowden, in this book, is confident that the years after 65 can be happy. He says that 'we are happiest, most fulfilled, if we are engaged in activities that are important to us, that demand, and receive, our commitment and time' (p74). The book shows that happiness after 65 is important to Bowden, and the book is testimony to his commitment and to the time he has devoted to it. Writing a book about happiness can be a fulfilling experience for one who is devoted to happiness.

This is not a "self-help" book. It is not *Finding Happiness after 65* but an 'exploration of happiness in old age' – a positive idea. It expects happiness, and explores it. The importance of happiness is traced through the ages, from the ancient Greece of Hippocrates and the early China of Confucius to the contemporary work of positive psychology, think tanks and business schools.

Variety, enthusiasm, passion – these are the features of a full life for Peter Bowden; they are important elements of happiness. The key message of this book is that happiness, a flourishing life, can be found after turning 65. You don't have to wait till 65, but there isn't some curtain or guillotine that comes down at 65 and cuts off any chance of further happiness. It is a book about life at full stretch. Ancient leaders, philosophers and teachers describe this in different ways. Peter Bowden makes an idiosyncratic selection, finding value in the flourishing life that Aristotle describes in the *Nicomachean Ethics*, in the complete person of the *junxi* in Confucius, and in the engagement of Seligman and the positive psychologists.

Bowden is a fan of books, and the positive impact of reading and writing shows. By drawing on many sources Bowden prompts the reader to look further, to dip anew into the writers who appear in the narrative. As I read the manuscript in preparation for writing this introduction a heap of books built up on my desk (and others on screen, for 'available online' is a frequent note in the text). Reading and reflection are active pursuits as this book persistently reminds us. Not only from the age of 65 onward. It is at the heart of learning and happiness. Bowden draws from Confucius, quoting from the very first lines in the *Analects*, 'Is it not a pleasure, having learned something, to try it out...?'.[1] It is as if the words of Cicero were coming true once again, over 2000 years later: 'To myself, indeed, the composition of this book has been so delightful, that it has not only wiped away all the annoyances of old age, but has even made it luxurious and delightful'.[2]

The book is an advertisement for books, perhaps in the tenor of the *Advertisement* that appears in Robert Burton's *The Anatomy of Melancholy*, the topic of chapter 4. That Bowden devotes a whole chapter in this present book to Burton's much reprinted seventeenth century work suggests that a search for similarities between them may not be in vain. So Burton's *Advertisement*, at the head of his volume, might speak to this current book as

> so valuable a repository of amusement and information...firmly supported by its own merit, and safe from the influence and blight of any future caprices of fashion. To open its valuable mysteries to those who have not had the advantage of a classical education...translations of the countless quotations from ancient writers... in all instances modernised.[3]

This modern book is a culmination of Peter Bowden's interest in ethics, in bringing about change that will make the world a better place. That commitment to action is apparent in Bowden's other post-65 activities, at least the ones I know about (there is a sailor in there somewhere, but I have very little experience of sailing, whether in small or large boats). It is *applied* ethics that interests Peter Bowden; a purely theoretical ethics, academic and philosophical, is in his mind less able to change the world for the better. So it was that he led a move to change the Constitution of the Australian Association for Professional and Applied Ethics so that its aims were more explicitly focused on change and action. So it was that he edited and championed a book entitled *Applied Ethics* with the subtitle 'strengthening ethical practices', a book that is about actual practice.

Happiness is not only personal it is also organisational, a feature of the community.[4] Bowden takes this as the basis for his assertion that happiness is, or should be, a focus for government action. As always, there is support in the ancients, both East and West, and in contemporary sources. There is also data, collected for the occasion, for the book is also built on two surveys which provide information about what it is that concerns people over 65 in Australia and what it is that makes them happy. Curiosity, especially curiosity prompted by a desire for greater understanding, is important not only for happiness but also for achievement, once again bringing Bowden's commitment to action and the achievement of good, making the world a better place, to the fore. The treatment in the book of meditation and reflection brings out one of its enduring messages, that it is within ourselves that happiness resides and that it is our own action that is important and we should be sceptical of those who say they have a cure, especially of those who promote a course. Bowden attended a number of meditation and well-being courses and reports his perceptions and experiences. Alongside those experiences he notes the importance of meditation in the Buddhist and Christian traditions, mentioning by name the great Spanish mystic Teresa of Avila, a woman at once practical in the reform of monasteries and thoughtful in seeking to understand the life of contemplation. Reflection, meditation and curiosity are all active, they are to a purpose.

When I first met Peter Bowden, I suspect he was already over 65. Both of us had begun our professional lives with a university degree in engineering, both had an interest in ethics supported by later study. We met at a conference of the Australian Association for Professional and Applied Ethics and later sat together on its executive committee. We are both engineers, who later took up formal pursuits in ethics, and thought it worth teaching to others.

Bowden suggests (p21) that the five ethical theories listed by Cicero as under discussion on Rome 45bc have grown into 20. If there is active discussion of 20 ethical theories in the world today, in the centres of government and at the heart of nations, that is to be applauded, but I doubt that there is that much debate. This book may prompt further discussion. Its author is certain, without doubt, and that will be a benefit for those confused by multitudinous and conflicting advice. There is something here to prompt a response, a call to engagement, a basis for meditation and reflection. Bowden makes it clear – chocolate, red wine, oysters and canned salmon are good for you…(p63). He sets out in the Afterword a solution to the quest for a single moral rule, a single ethical guideline, 'not to harm others. And if they are suffering harm, to help alleviate that harm in any way we see fit' (p97). His goal is to make the world a better place, and that is surely good.

Howard Harris
School of Management, University of South Australia
Adelaide, July 2018

FOREWORD

The original impetus for this book was a depression survey. If you have ever been given such a survey to complete, you will find the title very apt. Depression surveys are unbelievably depressing. A sample of the questions from different surveys is shown in Chapter 1. It is difficult to believe that the lives of some people are so sad that they would answer questions such as these in the affirmative. And, it would seem, older people are faced with more difficulties than they were in their earlier years – they have less money, their aches and pains are more frequent, they no longer contribute to society in the sense of a job that earns a living, and the grim reaper is not that far away. It appears that a bleak picture awaits an ageing population. A health clinic for oldies, run by a local hospital, which I had joined, sent me a depression survey. My reaction was one of sheer disbelief that anybody could feel so miserable. I believed totally the opposite. Hence this book.

That older people are more affected by depression is a widespread belief. The *Better Health* program of the Australian state government of Victoria has a program on depression in older people. Its website states that "it is thought that between 10 and 15 per cent of Australians over the age of 65 experience depression. Rates of depression among people living in residential aged care facilities are believed to be much higher than the general population – around 35 per cent."

They also published their finding that "On average, one in six people (one in five women and one in eight men) will experience depression at some stage of their lives".

The Black Dog Institute, a "not-for-profit organisation and world leader in the diagnosis, treatment and prevention of mood disorders such as depression and bipolar disorder" has a webpage devoted to identifying the signs of depression in older people. Symptoms include a loss of interest in life, lack of enjoyment in normal activities, apprehension, poor sleep, and persistent thoughts of death, chronic unexplained pain, poor concentration or impaired memory. One of its findings is that lifestyle changes in mid-life may avert the onset of depression.

This book, however, is not about depression. Or even curing it – although many of its findings may help prevent it. It is about happiness in old age. The research for the book started with the conviction that the years over 65 were in fact the happiest of your life; also that the assumption that older people were miserable was totally wrong. The book documents the explorations underlying the search for the reasons why the post 65 years can indeed be your best.

Three methods were used to find support for this assertion. The first method was direct interviews – asking people over 65 years of age whether they were more satisfied with their lives now than before they were 65. Sixty-five was seen as the break between work and retirement. The initial discussions were informal and quite extensive. Eventually they were structured in a survey sent to every person over 65 that I could locate. The objective of the survey was to obtain measurable results. It asked whether the respondent preferred life now to before he or she turned 65, and if the answer was a yes or no, then why. It questioned their preferences for life over 65 rather than ask about their happiness, or fulfilment or flourishing. It was thought that the answers to this question would be more considered, less subjective to the mood that respondents were in at the time they responded to the survey. A short summary of a fascinating series of answers is that a majority of people do agree that their years after they turn 65 are their best. They prefer their lives now than to earlier. The majority is not huge, but it is nevertheless, a majority. The reasons are many. The overriding one is that people over 65 are freer to do what they want to do, and that many have found activities that are totally satisfying and fulfilling.

The second method was to find out what the world had written on happiness over the last two thousand years. Our happiness has been an issue of great curiosity to the human race almost from the beginning of time. Starting with the Greek philosophers, Plato and Aristotle, along with Herodotus, a historian giving us the views of Solon, a Greek political leader, they provide us with a powerful introduction. The Romans followed them, particularly in the writings of Cicero, one of the more outstanding contributors to the thinking of the human race. Also included are the thoughts of the Asian philosophers, particularly Confucius, Mencius, and the Buddha.

The world's great intellects have since written on happiness over the centuries, ending with a brand-new discipline, positive psychology, which is less than 20 years old. Identifying the findings of the positive psychology movement became then the third method used to determine the contributions to our happiness. A fascinating finding is the extent to which this new discipline, utilising the techniques of the modern-day sciences, found answers that reinforced the earlier thoughts of Plato, Aristotle and Cicero, even Buddhism.

The surveys were usually organised through a formal body that catered for people over 65, such as a Probus (a worldwide association of clubs for retirees), the University of the Third Age or government support organisations for senior citizens. They were organised in the Eastern and Southern states of Australia. When organised through a group that could meet after completing the questionnaire (such as Probus or U3A), the findings were opened, analysed and reviewed with that group. This book then attempts to capture the essence of these findings and compare them with the thoughts and writing that had been developed over the centuries.

One of the early findings was that the word happiness is open to multiple interpretations. It can be that bubbly feeling when your enjoyment is at a very high level, to a contentment, even deep satisfaction with how your life is unfolding at this moment in time. In short, happiness has many paths, each of which set out in the later chapters. Nevertheless, there is an amazing congruence between the ancient philosophers and the modern psychologists. The findings of the surveys also support the ancient philosophers and the modern psychologists. But the agreement is not total. They are not one hundred percent in agreement with each other. There are some intriguing differences.

On a different note, it is to Greece that we owe the word melancholy - the word comes from the ancient Greek melas, "black", and kholé, "bile". It was considered as a distinct disease - a person whose constitution tended to have a preponderance of black bile had a melancholic disposition. Hippocrates, again a world's first, a physician, studied melancholy, issuing many pronouncements on its causes: "Grief and fear, when lingering, provoke melancholia," he tells us. Hippocrates conceived four fundamental personality types, sanguine (enthusiastic, active, and social), choleric (short-tempered, fast, or irritable), melancholic (analytical, wise, and quiet), and phlegmatic (relaxed and peaceful). Most personality formulations, including his, include a mixture of the personality types, where an individual shares two or more temperaments. This book is conceived as an antidote to one of Hippocrates' types: melancholic. It explores ways to achieve a happy, fulfilling life.

Aristotle wrote his book on happiness in 350 BC. He was not the first; his fellow countryman, Plato wrote *The Republic,* in 380 BC in which he spoke through Socrates, arguing that happiness is obtainable by human effort. Aristotle used the word eudaimonia to describe happiness, a word that has had philosophers and psychologists arguing for 2500 years. The argument is whether eudaimonia is best translated as happiness or whether words such as flourishing or fulfilment or well-being are more appropriate. This argument raises the question, what is happiness – a question on which this book endeavours to find an answer.

That goal then creates two subsidiary objectives: Firstly, once you determine what is a eudaimistic or happy life, then how do you achieve it? The second objective is whether older people can achieve that eudaimistic life. Within these objectives the book attempts to answer the question, if we are unhappy can we apply some of Socrates' human effort, or other lessons, to correct the problem?

The findings of the research can be presented in summary at this stage. The survey found that most people over sixty-five believe that their life is better now than it was, but it is not by a massive majority (87 Yes to 68 No). The positive reasons given by the respondents to the survey do in part reflect the development over the centuries of human thought on this topic. But the respondents also have some special reasons for their answers. Happiness is unique to each individual. Some universal rules were identified, but each of us is different, with often very different lives. The findings that emerged were in the context of each person who reported those findings. But they can be and were aggregated. Each reader will need to sort his or her own way through the lessons of history, both ancient and modern, and determine for him or herself, how those lessons are best applied. Help will be provided in later paragraphs in how best to apply those lessons.

One of the findings that appears in two of the research sources, is that our governments have some responsibility for our happiness. Plato said it in 400 BC; Cicero echoed him in 40 BC. Some of the Asian philosophies also agree. A number of the influential psychologists of the twenty-first century echo them in turn. The over 65 respondents do not mention this concern, but it is an issue with which they should be concerned. It is not an easy task on which to come to a clear-cut resolution on how governments might fulfil this obligation. An attempt has been made in the penultimate chapter, by examining the priorities of several think tanks around the world, supplemented by some research documented in the Afterword.

The book is set out in the three parts outlined above – the writings over history, the modern positive psychologists and then the findings from the questionnaire, supplemented by an examination of what possible future role of our governments could play in this process. All categories are, in a sense, independent third-party findings. In the final section, the author attempts to interpret the findings. This interpretation attempts to be impassionate and balanced. It is very difficult, if not impossible, to feel the need to write this book, and then to put in the months required for the survey discussions and to undertake the extensive reading over many centuries of human writing, without arriving at some conclusions on how we best ensure our happiness. This attempt at a balanced conclusion is set out in the final chapter.

The book incidentally, is of value to all ages, not only those who have reached 65 and beyond. Of the three sources of information, two – the writings over history and the modern-day psychologists, are relevant to people of all ages. The third, the findings from the questionnaire sent to those over 65, has several lessons of value to younger people. One lesson worth learning is to start early in preparing for a life after 65 that will be satisfying and fulfilling. Initiating habits and practices that were identified by the survey respondents, in midlife or even earlier, will be major contributors to a happy, healthy and long lasting old age.

An addendum to the foreword

A copy of the survey is reproduced in the chapter outlining the findings from the questionnaire. The respondents were Australian, located primarily in the eastern states, generally in the average middle-income brackets. Roughly equal numbers of men and women were surveyed. With 155 responses, we can draw some firm conclusions. But additional responses would give us a more reliable understanding of issues such as the differences in happiness attendant on place of birth or current residential location, on gender, even on income, or on age. Readers of this book who are over 65 are urged to go to the website *www.65plusthebestyearsofyourlife.net* and respond to the questionnaire. That website will be periodically updated with the research findings.

Chapter 1

UNHAPPINESS IN OLDER PEOPLE

This chapter may be the first in the book, but it could be skipped. It is intended to outline the reasons why the world thinks older people should not be all that happy. It outlines the research and depression surveys, some of which our older readers may already be familiar with.

The purpose of the chapter is to demonstrate to readers why the book was written: that it is soul destroying to realise that many people will answer yes to the questions in the depression surveys. This book is not about depression, it is about being happy, about what makes a fulfilling and satisfying life.

So if you do not want to read about unhappiness, skip this chapter.

It does include a depression survey that the reader can do online. If you do take the survey, and you find that you may be depressed, seek professional help. If you find that you have only a tendency that way – that life after 65 is not all that you hoped for, then read on.

The problems of old age have been recorded since time immemorial, from the days of Aristotle and Plato, even Cicero, and are familiar to all of us – a weakening body, loss of strength, a fading memory, increasing irrelevance in that you are no longer contributing to society, that you now need to be supported by the younger members of that society. Remember the commandment: "honour thy father and mother". It was designed to make sure our children looked after us in our old age.

The Journal *Current Opinions in Psychiatry* carries the statement: "depression is fast becoming a major public health problem throughout the world with a very high prevalence rate in the 65 and over age group"[1]

Andrew Dentino and his professional associates examined 1,686 rural and urban community-dwelling persons (aged 70+ yrs.)[2]. He found that the prevalence of depression increases with age.

The World Health Organisation tells us that with regard to age, suicide rates are highest in persons aged 70 years or over for both men and women in almost all regions of the world[3].

The Depression Tests

The three tests outlined in this chapter are commonly employed depression tests. The first is that of the Black Dog Institute, a manager of programs designed to create safer, mentally healthier work environments. Beyond Blue, an Australian depression assistance charity, is another. Both have a depression test on their websites on which you can score yourself. The Beyond Blue test is termed the "Anxiety and Depression Checklist (K10)".[4] This anxiety and depression checklist has a special section for older people, in which it states:

> *Depression is common throughout the Australian population, and older people are more likely to experience contributing factors such as physical illness or personal loss.*
> *It is thought that between 10 and 15 per cent of older people experience depression and about 10 per cent experience anxiety. Rates of depression among people living in residential aged-care are believed to be much higher, at around 35 per cent.*[5]

It also notes that common depressive symptoms, dementia or poor health, are incorrectly attributed to old age. But they are symptoms of depression – to be taken seriously.

Figure 1.1
Black Dog Institute

Little interest or pleasure in doing things?

Feeling down, depressed or hopeless?

Trouble falling or staying asleep or sleeping too much?

Feeling tired or having little energy?

Poor appetite or overeating?

Feeling bad about yourself – that you are a failure or have let yourself or your family down?

Trouble concentrating on things, such as reading the newspaper or watching television?

Moving or speaking so slowly that other people could have noticed?

Or the opposite – being so fidgety? or restless that you have been moving around a lot more than usual?

Thoughts that you would be better off dead, or of hurting yourself?

AGAINST WHICH YOU RATE YOURSELF

Not true   Slightly true   Moderately true   Very true

The Black Dog Institute on-line test is provided in Figure 1.1.[6] The author tried himself on this test and scored a "mild" depression, along with the suggestion that I talk to my doctor. Utter disbelief in this answer called for a retest. A more positive response on the amount of effort required to concentrate placed this occasionally absent-minded writer in the normal range.

The Geriatric Depression Test (Figure 1.2) is the test that this author was originally given, and that he found depressing. It was the test that started this book. It has questions such as "Do you feel pretty worthless the way you are now?" or "Do you often feel helpless?", If the answers are yes, you are doomed. Hopefully, this book will set you up with ideas that will enable you to answer these questions with a strong "NO".

**Figure 1.2
The Geriatric Depression Test**

1. Are you basically satisfied with your life?
2. Have you dropped many of your activities and interests?
3. Do you feel that your life is empty?
4. Do you often get bored?
5. Are you hopeful about the future?
6. Are you bothered by thoughts you can't get out of your head?
7. Are you in good spirits most of the time?
8. Are you afraid that something bad is going to happen to you?
9. Do you feel happy most of the time?
10. Do you often feel helpless?
11. Do you often get restless and fidgety?
12. Do you prefer to stay at home, rather than going out and doing new things?
13. Do you frequently worry about the future?
14. Do you feel you have more problems with memory than most?
15. Do you think it is wonderful to be alive now?
16. Do you often feel downhearted and blue?

17. Do you feel pretty worthless the way you are now?
18. Do you worry a lot about the past?
19. Do you find life very exciting?
20. Is it hard for you to get started on new projects?
21. Do you feel full of energy?
22. Do you feel that your situation is hopeless?
23. Do you think that most people are better off than you are?
24. Do you frequently get upset over little things?
25. Do you frequently feel like crying?
26. Do you have trouble concentrating?
27. Do you enjoy getting up in the morning?
28. Do you prefer to avoid social gatherings?
29. Is it easy for you to make decisions?
30. Is your mind as clear as it used to be?

A score > about 5 points is suggestive of depression and should warrant a follow up interview. Scores >10 are almost always depression
THIS TEST IS NOT FOR SELF SCORING

Chapter 2

THE EARLY PHILOSOPHERS

Issues of happiness have been a subject of human inquiry for 2500 years. The Greek historian, Herodotus, the world's first writer of history was, unbelievably, the first to lay out his concept of happiness in his *Histories* (written in 440 BC). He asked whether wealth or power make you happy. It is, as we will find out, a question that has been asked over several thousand years, and that is still asked today. Herodotus' responses are set out below.

Hippocrates (c. 460 – c. 370 BC), the world's first physician, was another who has contributed to the thoughts gathered in this book, but this time on sadness, or melancholy.

Deserving of particular mention are two Greek philosophers, often termed the fathers of philosophy, Aristotle and Plato, who also wrote on happiness. It is to Aristotle that we most owe the structure of this book. His word, eudaimonia, often translated as happiness, has caused much discussion over the years. Whether it is best translated as a joyous time, such as portrayed by Pollyanna, the cheerful orphan who brought happiness and joy into her small village - subject of a 1960 Walt Disney movie that earned Hayley Mills an Oscar. Or whether it is best translated as fulfilment - the longer-term achievement of deeply satisfying ambition; or whether it is simply the striving for this achievement. A fourth translation is well-being. A search on the web will identify several well-being institutes who will set out their approaches for achieving happiness, security, safety, fulfilment, or perhaps even prosperity.

A later chapter of this book sets out the survey that the author made on happiness in older people, and their responses. Rather than ask people whether they were happy, and where on this spread of the above possible translations they would fit. The question that was asked was whether they preferred life now, after 65, to life before and the reasons behind their preferences. This approach was intended to provide a more reliable and measurable response, better able to give some guidelines from which we could draw actionable conclusions.

Aristotle wrote his book on happiness in 350 BC. Aristotle's fellow countryman and former teacher, Plato, wrote *The Republic*, in 380 BC in which he spoke, through Socrates, arguing that happiness is obtainable by human effort. If through our own efforts we can find happiness (or fulfilment, etc.), then it would be worthwhile for us determining where we direct these efforts.

Herodotus set out, in the first recorded history of western humanity, his beliefs on whether wealth or power makes you happy. In his *Histories*, he wrote on happiness even earlier than Plato (who lived about 428–348 BC) or Aristotle (384–322 BC). His assertion is that wealth or power do not make you happy. His reasons are given in his recounting of a meeting between Croesus (595 – c. 546 BC), King of Lydia, an independent kingdom in what is now the Western part of Turkey, and Solon, a leading Athenian thinker and politician. Solon (about 638 – 558 BC) is often credited with having laid the foundations for democracy, first achieved in ancient Greece.

Herodotus records that Croesus, famed for his riches, asked Solon: "Who is the happiest man you have ever seen?" In the words of Herodotus: "This he asked because he thought himself the happiest of mortals: but Solon answered him without flattery, and as he actually believed: "Tellus of Athens, sire."

The king was quite taken aback and demanded to know how such a common man might be considered the happiest of all. Tellus, Solon replied, had lived in a city with a government that allowed him to prosper. He had fine sons, who had in turn given him many grandchildren, all of whom survived into young adulthood. After enjoying a contented life, he fought and died on the battlefield when the Athenians had a war against their neighbours in Eleusis. He was given the honour of a public funeral by his fellow Athenians.

Croesus, disconcerted, asked who was the next happiest. Solon's answer was Cleobis and Biton - two young men who had enjoyed success at the Athenian games, and who carried their mother to the temple of Hera to celebrate the goddess' festival.

Solon explained that while the rich did have advantages over the poor – "the means to bear calamity and satisfy their appetites" – they had no monopoly on the things that were truly valuable in life: civic service, raising healthy children, being self-sufficient, having a sound body, and honouring the gods and one's family. In addition, riches tend to create more issues for their bearers – more money, along with which came more problems.

Plato (c. 428– 348 BC)

Plato, who was founder of the Academy in which Aristotle studied and worked, has much to say about happiness, virtue, and political life in his book, *The Republic*. His findings on happiness are also found in another of his dialogues, *The Euthydemus*, as well as *The Republic*. In this latter work, through the words of Socrates, he puts creating peoples' happiness as one of the functions of government:

> *Our object in the construction of the state is the greatest happiness of the whole, and not that of any one class.* (The Republic, Book IV).

It is a laudable objective, and one that found some support from Cicero, five hundred years later, as well as in the work of some of the modern researchers on positive psychology. Martin Seligman is generally regarded as the father of this new discipline, but the psychologist who puts the greatest emphasis on the role of government in ensuring our happiness is Richard Layard, program director of the Centre for Economic Performance at the London School of Economics. But in both ancient Greece and in our modern democracies, the overriding and yet unanswered question is what are the ways in which government can contribute to our happiness. Considerable disagreement on this question was evident then and it is certainly evident now.

In Plato's case, he argued that his version of the utopian society required each of the classes of inhabitants - philosophers, warriors, and workers – to have pre-assigned roles. Governance was in the hands of those best qualified for that responsibility, the "Philosopher Kings" as Plato labelled them. Each inhabitant is educated for their specific role. They also share as much as possible, with wives, children, and property in common.

Aristotle argued that this arrangement is not natural, as people have different talents and ambitions. It is in this part of his response that Aristotle uses the phrase "man is by nature a political animal." It is difficult not to agree with Aristotle; that to be constrained into one of the three possible boxes offered by Plato would create a very boring life.

As readers of this book will also discover, this author has some degree of scepticism on the ability of philosophers to develop practical answers to everyday questions. This belief is not universal. Hakan Tell in Harvard University's Center for Hellenic Studies asserts that Plato's articulation of philosophy was so powerful that it remained largely uncontested into modern times[1]. Philosopher kings, this writer believes, would be a disaster. Plato however, in *Euthydemus*, places wisdom as a foundation for happiness, not the state. As we are supposed to gain wisdom as we get older, this path to happiness should create no difficulty for older people. However, as we progress into the research of the modern positive psychologists, it will be found that the progression via wisdom is not all that straightforward a process. Positive psychology, it will be remembered, is a relatively recent branch of psychology: "the scientific study of what makes life most worth living"[2].

Aristotle (384–322 BC)

Aristotle was a Greek scientist and philosopher. According to the Encyclopædia Britannica: "Aristotle was the first genuine scientist in history ... every scientist is in his debt." He is claimed not only to be the founder of psychology, but a significant contributor to political science, logic, poetics, physics and biology. He is also claimed as the first psychologist by the modern-day psychologists.

Aristotle joined Plato's Academy in Athens in 364 BC. Plato died in 347 BC, but Aristotle did not follow him as leader. He was appointed tutor to Alexander the Great in 343 BC. In 335 BC, Aristotle returned to Athens, establishing there his own school, the Lyceum. His work, at that stage, had already begun to digress from Plato, turning more to empirical research, away from speculative philosophy. He was a brilliant man, and along with Cicero, one of the few genuine greats in our early human history.

Only a fraction of Aristotle' works have survived. Even then, they cover an amazing range of investigative effort. One of them is on happiness. He wrote in *Nichomachean Ethics* (350 BC):

> *He is happy who lives in accordance with complete virtue and is sufficiently equipped with external goods, not for some chance period but throughout a complete life.*

In short, Aristotle is arguing that one essence of a happy life is a virtuous life. It is a finding endorsed by several of today's positive psychologists. But an issue which is explored in the Afterword is defining what we mean by being virtuous. Also, to be happy Aristotle has said that we need to be "sufficiently equipped" with the world's goods. Our survey of the over 65s endorsed this conclusion. You cannot be poor. Modern research has confirmed this finding. It has found that men working in the lowest-skilled occupations had a 44 per cent higher risk of suicide than the male average[3]. The relationship between poverty and happiness is an acute issue. The need for at least a reasonable income is one of the reasons why one conclusion from this book is that we need to start early on the quest for happiness. It also has an impact on our conclusions on the role of government.

Neel Burton, writing in *Psychology Today* states that Aristotle also acknowledges that our good or bad fortune can play a part in determining our happiness. For example, Aristotle states that happiness can be affected by such factors as our material circumstances, our place in society, and even our looks. Yet he maintains that by living our life to the full according to our essential nature as rational beings, we are bound to become happy regardless.[4]

The development of human thought on the two issues of happiness and virtue over the following centuries is outlined in the subsequent chapters. It should be mentioned that today's positive psychologists have also adopted Aristotle's two issues of happiness and virtue. They have done so, however, with variations and additions that reflect the research methodology of the twenty first century.

Aristotle identified twelve virtues, listed in Figure 2.1. He provided a description of each virtue, locating it between an excess and a deficiency. A reader may not agree with each virtue, or whether the excess or deficiency applies in a 21st century democracy. Aristotle's courage, for instance, is courage in war. It is modified by his concept of nobility, discussed below. Many today, however, would put courage to fight for a deeply held moral principle ahead of courage in war.

One virtue that has stood the test of time, however, is temperance. A virtue esteemed by religious thinkers, philosophers, and more recently, the 21st century psychologists, it is a cardinal virtue in Greek philosophy and in Christianity, as well as in Buddhism and Hinduism. Temperance, one of the six virtues in the positive psychology movement, is included with wisdom, courage, humanity, justice, and transcendence. Generally considered as control over excess, it is evidenced by behaviours of chastity, modesty, prudence, self-regulation, forgiveness and mercy. Each of which involves restraining an excess of behaviour, such as sexual desire, vanity, or anger.

Figure 2.1
Aristotle's 12 virtues

Vice of Deficiency	Virtuous Mean	Vice of Excess
Cowardice	Courage	Rashness
Insensibility	Temperance	Intemperance
Illiberality	Liberality	Prodigality
Pettiness	Munificence	Vulgarity
Humble-mindedness	High-mindedness	Vaingloriness
Want of Ambition	Right Ambition	Over-ambition
Spiritlessness	Good Temper	Irascibility
Surliness	Friendly Civility	Obsequiousness
Ironical Depreciation	Sincerity	Boastfulness
Boorishness	Wittiness	Buffoonery
Shamelessness	Modesty	Bashfulness
Callousness	Just Resentment	Spitefulness

The role of government in ensuring our happiness has been ascribed to Plato. When we read the section on Cicero, we will discover that he also advocates that a role of government is to ensure the happiness of its people. It is also a thought endorsed by the modern psychologists 2000 years later. Aristotle does not make this precise assertion, but he does imply it. He writes in his *Politics* that "the truly democratic statesman must study how the multitude may be saved from extreme poverty", and that "measures must be contrived that bring lasting justice to all".[5] It is little wonder that Cicero wrote of Aristotle that his work "was like the pouring out of gold." Plutarch uses the phrase "like a river of flowing gold".

Aristotle' concept of nobility, of wisdom, is uplifting. It is a concept that we would all like to see in our politicians, even in our leaders of industry. In adversity, Aristotle claims, nobility shines through, when "a man endures repeated and severe misfortune with patience, not owing to insensibility but from generosity and greatness of soul." He lists a dozen strengths that we see in the wise and noble soul:

- The pleasures arising from thinking and learning will make us think and learn all the more.
- Without friends, no one would want to live, even if he had all other goods.
- The wise man does not expose himself needlessly to danger since there are few things about which he cares sufficiently;

- But he is willing, in great crises, to give even his life--knowing that under certain conditions it is not worthwhile to live;
- He is of a disposition to do men service, though he is ashamed to have a service done to him;
- To confer a kindness is a mark of superiority; to receive one is a mark of subordination;
- Does not take part in public displays;
- He is open in his dislikes and preferences;
- He is not fond of talking... It is no concern of his that he should be praised, or that others should be blamed;
- Is never fired with admiration...nothing is great in his eyes;
- He cannot live in complaisance with others, except it be a friend; complaisance is the characteristic of a slave;
- He never feels malice, and always forgets and passes over injuries;
- He does not speak evil of others, even of his enemies, unless it be directly to them;
- His carriage is sedate, his voice deep, his speech measured; he is not given to hurry, for he is concerned about only a few things;
- He is not prone to vehemence, for he thinks no issue is that important;
- He bears the accidents of life with dignity and grace, making the best of his circumstances, like a skilful general.

Although this writer's admiration of this Greek philosopher/scientist does shine through in these pages, it must be recorded that Aristotle also had some weaknesses. His work was designed for upper class educated Greek males. He does not write for the working classes, nor for women or slaves. Learning and curiosity are also (surprisingly) minimised as one of his virtues. This, despite that learning and curiosity were perhaps Aristotle's greatest virtues. He apparently did not consider them as a virtue for other members of his community. As we move into the thinking of the twenty-first century, these two attributes will assume a much higher importance in achieving a happy life. Another comment we might make on Aristotle's virtues is his failure to condemn harming others. In fact, by promoting courage in war as a virtue, he is indirectly encouraging war. As we move through the pages of this book, and especially in the Afterword, a case will be made that the most powerful virtue of all is not harming others; in fact, by helping others when needed.

Magnificence (at times) includes a person who big notes himself and is another questionable attribute that Aristotle praises: "Power & wealth are desirable for the honour that they bring".

He also had some observations in his *On Youth and Old Age*. We may not like them, but we must admit to some underlying truths:

- The elderly live by memory rather than hope.
- They have a lot of experience, are sure about nothing and under-do everything.
- They are small-minded because they have been humbled by life. Driven too much by the useful; not enough by the noble.
- They are cynical and distrustful and neither love warmly nor hate bitterly.
- They are not shy.

Aristotle's attributes are not all that flattering of older people. We will determine in the coming chapters whether we can find nobler character traits for those over 65.

Aristotle differs from the modern researchers in his assessment of the impact that being virtuous has on eudaimonia in several important respects. So it is of value to find out what Aristotle meant by virtue.

Aristotle had set out his concepts on virtue, and on nobility, in *Nichomachean Ethics*. Readers will note that modern researchers have identified 24 character strengths and virtues (set out in the later chapter on positive psychology) that "enable individuals and communities to thrive". Positive psychology, discussed in Chapter 6 under modern psychological research on happiness, is founded on the belief that "people want to lead meaningful and fulfilling lives, to cultivate what is best within themselves, and to enhance their experiences of love, work, and play." Aristotle's thoughts on virtues and nobility have much in common with the modern-day character strengths.

Aristotle also wrote on youth and old age. His thoughts were set out in a relatively short treatise with three titles, *On Youth and Old Age, On Life and Death, On Breathing*. They are available on-line. In these pieces, Aristotle sets out his belief that we have a soul, which he locates in the heart.

Thucydides

Thucydides was not a philosopher, but a historian who also wrote on happiness. He was born in Alimos, 8 km south of Athens about 455 B.C. He died between 411 and 400 B.C. He is known for his *History of the Pelopon-*

nesian War, which records the war between Sparta and Athens in the 5th Century BC. His history includes the dialogue in which Athens and the Melos leaders negotiate the possible surrender of Melos, a Greek island in the Aegean Sea. Melos is the most southwestern island in the Cyclades group. Melos surrendered in the winter of 416 or 415 BC. The Athenian invaders executed the adult men and sold the women and children into slavery. They also settled 500 of their own colonists on the island. Sparta recaptured the island in 405 BC, when Athens lost the war. Athenian cruelty on Melos is noted is several subsequent Greek accounts of the affair. The Greek historian Xenophon in 405 BC, with the Spartan army closing in on Athens, wrote that the people of Athens were worried that the Spartans would treat them with the same cruelty that the Athenian army had shown the Melians.

Thucydides' phrase "The secret of happiness is freedom, and the secret of freedom, courage" is often quoted, but it is suspected that his happiness (for which he used the word eudaimonia) is not the same eudaimonia that of Aristotle. It is sometimes translated as prosperity. The phrase appears on several self- help websites, intended to convey the message that with courage you can help yourself and thus will eventually be free. The words also appear on many war memorials, signifying freedom from foreign conquest as a happy state.

The Asian Philosophers

How to achieve happiness is a philosophical issue. Philosophy has, over the centuries, been dominated by Western philosophers. Witness, for instance, Bertrand Russell's *A History of Western Philosophy*. But the Asian philosophers have made their statements on this issue and should be recorded. This section attempts to do that. First, however, it should be noted that many of the Western philosophers place the practice of virtue as a prime requirement for happiness. Virtue, however, has many meanings. It ranges from the upright manly behaviour of well brought up Greek gentlemen to behaving honestly, or with sympathy and compassion. The Afterword to this book attempts to define virtue. It draws on both Western and Eastern philosophies in the attempt. It is put as an afterword as it is a philosophical essay only partly aligned with happiness. The eastern philosophies are Hinduism, the Jains, and Buddhism[6]. The afterword also draws on four of the Western moral philosophies. To relieve the reader of the need to jump ahead to an afterword, it might be mentioned that the definition reached there uses the words of the Dalai Lama, "Our prime duty in life is to help others; at least not to harm them".

Confucius

Kung Fu-tzu (the Master Kung) known to the West by the Jesuit translation, Confucius, lived in China from 551 – 479 BC. China then consisted of a number of small feudal states, which, although subject to the kings of the Zhou Dynasty, were independent in practice. He was born in Shandong Province, near present-day Qufu, to the North East of China.

His teachings were compiled in the Analects, many years after his death. The opening lines of the Analects reflect his views on happiness "Isn't it a pleasure to acquire knowledge and to constantly to exercise oneself therein?"[7] These words embody the findings of the positive psychologists of the 21st. century, encapsulated by them in the word "curiosity." Extravagant enjoyments or stimulating amusements were harmful, according to the Analects. His teachings, however, are mainly moral in nature. They emphasized personal and governmental morality, correct social relationships, and justice.

His emphasis on government reflects another finding from later in this book. From the early Greek philosophers, through Cicero, to several of the modern-day psychologists, emphasis is placed on the obligation of the government to ensure the happiness of its people. There is far from uniform agreement on how this obligation is fulfilled. In Confucius' case it is being trustworthy and honest in the handling of public affairs, economical in managing expenditures, loving of the people, using them only as appropriate, establishing regulations and keeping order through punishments. Providing leadership is also a requirement.

Mencius

Mencius (385–302 BC) was a Chinese philosopher widely regarded as a Confucian disciple. His thoughts are sufficiently deep for him to be described as the "Second Sage", after Confucius himself. He was a contemporary of Plato, born, however, on the other side of the world, in Shandong province, somewhat near Confucius' birthplace. During the Warring States period (403–221 BC), Mencius was an official and scholar at the Jixia Academy in the State of Qi.

The Jesuits, who had translated the work of Confucius, also translated that of Mencius, although with less commitment. One, Matteo Ricci, the first European to enter Beijing, objected to Mencius's condemnation of celibacy as unfilial, Mencius' reason was that you were not observing a commitment to your parents to carry on the family, the family name, to provide children and grandchildren, who not only give you pleasure but who would look after you in your old age. The Confucian commitment to honouring family ancestors was likewise an aspect of some controversy, as it was deemed incompatible with Catholic religious beliefs. The Chinese Confucian practice of honouring family ancestors was considered incompatible with Catholic belief. The Jesuits argued that these Chinese rites were secular rituals compatible with Christianity. The Dominicans and Franciscans disagreed. In 1704 pope Clement XI banned the rites, with Benedict XIV reaffirming the ban in 1742. Pope Pius XII issued a decree on December 8, 1939, authorizing Chinese Catholics to observe the ancestral rites and participate in Confucius-honouring ceremonies.

Mencius is primarily a moral scholar and has little to say on happiness. One Western scholar, Chris Fraser, notes how little the texts in classical Chinese philosophy have to say about happiness in the philosophical thought of the early fifth to late third centuries BC.[8]

Fraser further states that conceptions of the excellent or flourishing human life are not topics central in the way that eudaimonia is in Greek thought, nor as psychological happiness is in classical utilitarianism, nor in the search for happiness as in much contemporary psychology. Classical Chinese ethics generally does not focus on the individual's happiness, whether in the psychological or well-being sense nor treat it as a central or highest good.

Ethics and happiness are central issues, however, as continually emphasised in this book. The role of virtue, and that of government, entwined with human nature, are continually encountered in Chinese writing. One of Mencius' stories, for example, is to emphasize the conflicting nature of human emotions. Mencius asserted that not even the most hardened and unsympathetic person would be unaffected when a nearby child fell down a well. He (or she) would try to help.

A happiness blog, nevertheless, describes Mencius as "the pioneer of Positive Psychology. He lays unprecedented emphasis on human nature and the role of the mind in the quest for happiness[9].

The Buddha, Buddhism and the Dalai Lama

Buddhism is not the fastest growing religion in the world, Islam is (due to high fertility rates, not conversions). it, however, attracts considerable interest in the Western countries. In Australia, according to its Bureau of Statistics, Buddhism is the fastest-growing spiritual tradition in the country in terms of percentage gain, with a growth of 79.1% for the period 1996 to 2001 (200,000→358,000).

There were 495 million Buddhists in the world in 2010, most of whom were in Asia. It is the world's fourth-largest religion.

It is debatable whether Buddhism is a religion, or a philosophy. If the former, it has no god. It has temples where its adherents gather, but they are not there for worship. They are there to listen to the discussions and the lectures by the Buddhist priests. Buddhism also has monasteries (for training young priests), stupas (memorials to the Buddha), and pagodas (temples).

Buddhism was founded by the Gautama Buddha, born of possibly royal parents in 563 BC or 623BC in North India near the modern Nepal-India border. In the years in between, it has grown into perhaps eighteen or more different subsects, as the Buddhas followers have placed their own interpretations on the teachings of the Buddha. The main schools are Theravada, literally "the Teaching of the Elders" or "the Ancient Teaching," Mahāyāna, literally the "Great Vehicle." Mahāyāna itself split between the traditional Mahāyāna teachings and the Vajrayāna teachings. There is also Zen Buddhism, an offshoot of Mahayana Buddhism. This book will not attempt to explain all the schools of Buddhism, only bring out the main tenets, and the impact they may have on happiness.

It is perhaps first worth noting, however, why so many versions of Buddhism have arisen. After the death of the Buddha, his disciples gathered to record his teachings. They recorded by memory, which would in itself introduce distortions. Centuries later, a second meeting took place. Over the years, new interpretations had crept in, thus creating the many versions of the Buddha's teaching. But there are common cores, which shall be presented first, for they have an impact on how we view happiness.

An overriding concept in Buddhism is the four noble truths – the concept that at the root cause of unhappiness in the world is suffering, Duhkha is the first noble truth. The second noble truth is desirous attachment, or greed - not getting what you want, encountering what you dislike, losing what you want. Overcoming dukkha is by stopping this clinging and attachment. That is the third noble truth – The need to cease, or overcome, the craving. The fourth noble truth is the approach to achieving the cessation of suffering. The Buddha prescribes The Eightfold Path as the treatment for our illness.

The eightfold path is a little complex, and perhaps a little over the top for most readers. But it has some core lessons within it and it worth repeating

Right view: Understanding that the Four Noble Truths provide you with insights into yourself and your feelings about yourself

Right thought: Resolving to do something about it

Right speech: Avoiding slander, gossip, lying, and all falsehoods and abusive speech.

Right conduct: Adhering to the concept of nonviolence (ahimsa), as well as refraining from any form of stealing or other impropriety. Also helping those who need our help

Right living: Making a living in an honest and ethical manner. This Buddhist guideline introduces the concept of Corporate Social Responsibility, 2000 years before it appeared. This concept states that businesses are an integral part of society should behave as morally and as ethically as everyday citizens are obliged.

Right effort: Avoiding negative thoughts and emotions, such as anger and jealousy.

Right mindfulness: This guideline is the origin of the Buddhist commitment to meditation. It compromises a reflective examination of our mental state and bodily health along with our concerns and feelings.

Right concentration: Reaching enlightenment. What is enlightenment? Buddhists tell us that it is reaching that understanding of yourself to the stage that you know yourself, that you are at peace with yourself. One of the yes answers to the over 65 survey for a positive outlook on life was self – acceptance, that you are no longer worried about what you think of yourself, or what other people think of you. It would seem that those gave this answer have reached the stage of a Buddhist enlightenment.

It would appear to this writer that the eightfold path of the Buddha is a series of major steps forward in coming to grips with our duhkha – our problems in life. But it does not reach the whole way. There are many problems and difficulties we face that are external to us – that come from outside - sickness and ill health being among them. The death of a loved one being another. Then there is war. Millions of people are faced with considerable suffering due to war.

The Dalai Lama, in conversation with Archbishop Desmond Tutu, faced this problem. In a meeting in Dharamsala in North India, headquarters of the Tibetan government in exile and the residence of the Dalai Lama, they invited questions on joy from around the world prior to the meeting. The two would answer the questions as best they could[10]. The most asked question was "how we could possibly live with joy in a world filled with suffering? Their answer is in the chapter titled "Despair: the world is in such a turmoil". This writer does not think they answered the question.

They did point out the ever-continuing improvements in the condition of the human race – the ending of slavery, the rights of women, the willingness of volunteers to go to help out in places of great danger. These moves will, in the long term, reduce suffering. But it does not seem possible that it can be permanently eliminated. It is a question that one of the respondents to the survey asked. It is also a question that Cicero asked, 2000 years ago. Cicero's answer, set out in a section, *Difficulties of Life* in Chapter 8, is yes, it is possible, although he has some doubts. Cicero draws mainly on Stoic thoughts.

Chapter 3

MARCUS TULLIUS CICERO

One intervening writer between the Greeks and relatively modern times is Marcus Tullius Cicero, a Roman lawyer, politician and writer, who lived from 106 to 43 B.C. He studied at Plato's academy, which was still in operation in Athens. He also formally educated his son at the Academy in Athens (although at times upbraiding him for not studying hard enough).

Cicero was killed the year after the assassination of Julius Caesar, on the orders of Mark Antony, in the struggles for power that overtook Rome. Cicero, a powerful public speaker, advocated a return to the old order – the Roman Republic, whereas Antony was one of the contenders for power, along with Augustus, in the second Triumvirate which marked the end of the Republic. (Marcus Aemilius Lepidus, a close ally of Julius Caesar, was the third member). Cicero was killed by the soldiers of Antony, and his head and hand were cut off and put on public exhibition in Rome. Despite his appearance as the hero of several Hollywood romances, Antony comes through in history, including in Plutarch's (45 -120 AD) lives of famous Romans, as a far from admirable person. Shakespeare, in his *Antony and Cleopatra* invests them both with "tragic grandeur." It is Cleopatra, however, that is awarded the grandeur:

> *Age cannot wither her, / Nor custom stale/ Her infinite variety*
> (Act II, scene ii)

John Adams, second President of the United States (1797–1801) and the first Vice President (1789–97) under George Washington, was heavily influenced by Cicero's writing. Adams worked with Thomas Jefferson in drafting the Declaration of Independence in 1776. He stated in the preface to *A Defence of the Constitutions of Government* (1787) that we need to pay attention to Cicero:

> As all the ages of the world have not produced a greater statesman and philosopher united in the same character, his authority should have great weight.

Adams was the first US president to reside in the White House. His son, John Quincey Adams, was the sixth US president.

The US Declaration of Independence endorses Cicero's statement on encouraging happiness as a role of government. It states:

> We hold these truths to be self-evident, that all men are created equal, that they are endowed by their Creator with certain unalienable rights. That among these are life, liberty and the pursuit of happiness.

As to who, Jefferson or Adams, was the originator of this commitment to happiness in 1776, is subject to some differences of opinion. Jefferson declared himself an Epicurean - a philosophical doctrine that advocates the pursuit of happiness. Other contenders include John Locke who wrote in his *Essay Concerning Human Understanding* that "the highest perfection of intellectual nature lies in a careful and constant pursuit of true and solid happiness". Even the Harvard Business Review has an article on happiness.[1]

Cicero on happiness and the role of government

Cicero earns a chapter in this book independently of other theorists for two reasons. One has been his endorsement that one role of government is to ensure peoples' happiness. A second reason is that he gave us advice relevant to happiness in old age.

In *De Legibus*, Cicero wrote, "Let the welfare of the people be the ultimate law".

'We are not born for ourselves alone'. This is also Cicero's message in *De Officiis*, his final and most popular work. In it, Cicero writes on how one can be an honourable statesman and constantly work for the good of the nation.

His major statement, however, is in *De Re Publica* [On the Republic], in which he clearly states that the role of government is to ensure peoples' happiness.

> ...as the purpose of a pilot is to ensure the smooth passage of his ship... so a statesman's objective must be the happiness of his country.

When we move forward two thousand years, we find that several of today's positive psychologists also assert that human happiness is an overriding function of government. Deciding how we do that, however, is not a simple task. It first requires us to decide what happiness is and then to define what governments can do to work towards its achievement. This is an issue which we will explore once we have the results of the questionnaire on what makes people happy.

Cicero defines happiness

Cicero's recommendations on happiness can be found in several of his writings:

> *That which stands first, and is most to be desired by all happy, honest and healthy-minded men, is dignified leisure.* From "Pro Publio Sestio":

> *"We cannot enjoy life if we spend our time and energy worrying about what happened yesterday and what will happen tomorrow. A happy life consists in tranquillity of mind.* In "On the Nature of the Gods".

Cicero also asserts that a virtuous life leads to happiness. He considers theological questions in his book, De *Natura Deorum,* as well as in his discourse *De Divinatione.* A rigorous examination of Cicero's beliefs on religion draws no firm conclusions, however, for it identifies passages where he apparently believes in morality and even in an afterlife, and others where he assigns the question of a religion to his wife, Terrentia.[2] Religion is a question discussed in Chapter 6, for modern research has found connections between religion, some forms of virtue and longevity.

Another of the many worthwhile writings by Cicero is *De finibus bonorum et malorum* ("On the ends of good and evil"), a philosophical work on ethics. It consists of five books, in which Cicero explains the philosophical views of Epicureanism, Stoicism, and the Platonism of Antiochus of Ascalon. The book was developed in the summer of the year 45 BC and dedicated to Marcus Junius Brutus, one of the leaders of the assassination of Caesar the following year. The fifth book describes a perfectly happy life, which includes both virtue and external goods, as the highest good. It is Cicero's thoughts on stoicism, and how one responds to adversity, that has the greatest value. It is an issue of some significance to older people, as the aches and pains of the advancing years increase. The book is significant in that it explains and discusses the main ethical theories under discussion in Rome. The five that Cicero discusses have since grown into many more, well in excess of perhaps twenty that have been developed over the years in between then and now.[3]

Cicero also wrote on friendship:

Friendship improves happiness, and abates misery, by doubling our joys, and dividing our grief. From *Laelius de Amicitia* ("Laelius on Friendship").

Cicero's thoughts on friendship have been recorded here as this book's survey of today's over 65s also reveals that friends are regarded as a source of happiness.

Cicero on old age

Cicero's contention for inclusion in this analysis of happiness in old age, however, lies primarily in his one work on old age itself. The advice is relevant today, 2000 years later, as it was in Cicero's time. In the last but one year of his life, Cicero, 63, writing as 84-year-old Cato the Elder, produced *De Senectute*...On Old Age. He found "four reasons why old age appears to be unhappy".

1. First, that it withdraws us from active pursuits;
2. Second, that it makes the body weaker (especially memory);
3. Third, that it deprives us of almost all physical pleasures; and,
4. Fourth, that it is not far removed from death.

All of which any of us will agree with. But Cicero had his responses to each of his own complaints against old age:

1. "Withdrawal from activities: It is not by muscle, speed, or physical dexterity that great things are achieved, but by reflection, force of character, and judgment; in these qualities old age is usually not ... poorer ... is even richer. That is also a belief of this book. He adds: "Of course (your body and memory weaken), if you do not exercise it.
2. "I certainly never heard of any old man forgetting where he had hidden his money! The aged remember everything that interests them, their appointments to appear in court, and who are their creditors and who their debtors.
3. "It is our duty...to resist old age; to compensate for its defects by a watchful care; to fight against it as we would fight against disease; to adopt a regimen of health; to practice moderate exercise; and to take just enough of food and drink to restore our strength and not to overburden it. Old age lacks the heavy banquet, the loaded table, and the oft-filled cup; therefore, it also lacks drunkenness, indigestion, and loss of sleep.

4. 'Death should be held of no account. For clearly (the impact of) death is negligible if it utterly annihilates the soul, or is even desirable, if it conducts the soul to some place where it is to live forever. What, then, shall I fear, if after death I am destined to be either not unhappy or happy?"

Some further information on Cicero and his thoughts are worth mentioning: First, he had no definite opinion on the soul – whether it was immortal or whether it died with the body, an issue on which Plato and Aristotle disagreed. This may seem a small point, but most of the world's religions believe that we have a soul and that it is immortal.

Secondly, his 44 BC recommendations to take exercise and eat healthily should sound very familiar to a reader in the 21st century. Cicero was not altogether the first, however. "Let food be thy medicine and medicine be thy food," was a statement made by Hippocrates (c. 460 –370 BC), the world's first physician. The statement at least implies that eating well will bring a healthy life.

Finally, he introduces the next chapter, on melancholy, Cicero did have some sad moments. "Would that he had been able to endure prosperity with greater self-control and adversity with more fortitude!" wrote C. Asinius Pollio, a contemporary Roman statesman and historian.[4]

Chapter 4

THE ANATOMY OF MELANCHOLY

The jump from Cicero to a group of modern philosophers - Mill, Russell and Darwin, must be interrupted by a digression to a book on melancholy *The Anatomy of Melancholy,* published by an Oxford clergyman, Robert Burton, in 1621, and the role of melancholy in happiness generally.

Many sociologists, psychologists and social critics tell us that the rapid spread of problems such as depression, stress and burnout are consequences of modernity and its challenges. They assert that a return to an earlier, simpler life will be beneficial. Anna Schaffer, Reader in Medical Humanities at the University of Kent tells us however: "Those who imagine that life in the past was simpler, slower and better are wrong. The experience of exhaustion, and anxieties about ... the wider population, are not bound to a particular time and place".

Melancholy has a history. From the Ancient Greek melas, "black", and kholé, "bile", melancholia was described as a distinct disease. A person whose constitution tended to have a preponderance of black bile had a melancholic disposition.

Hippocrates in his Aphorisms, 400 BC wrote

> *But if the autumn be northerly and dry, it agrees well with persons of a humid temperament, and with women; but others will be subject ... in some cases to melancholy.*

Hippocrates also wrote:

> *Grief and fear, when lingering, provoke melancholia.*

Lucius Annaeus Seneca, or Seneca the Younger, a Roman stoic philosopher, also wrote on unhappiness. In 41 AD, Seneca was sentenced to exile on Corsica for a possible affair with Julia Livilla, sister to Caligula and Agrippina. Helvia, Seneca's mother, had been marked by unimaginable loss — her own mother had died while giving birth to Helvia. She outlived her husband, her uncle, and three of her grandchildren. Twenty days after one the grandchildren — Seneca's own son — died in her arms, Helvia received news that Seneca had been sentenced to life in exile. His *Consolation to Helvia*, available online, has many thoughts on managing sadness. Perhaps the most significant is the Stoic statement: *Everlasting misfortune does have one blessing, that it ends up by toughening those whom it constantly afflicts.*

Stoic philosophy calls for a life lived 'in accordance with nature'. It believes in the restraint of animal instincts and the severing of emotional ties. These beliefs were formulated by the followers of Zeno of Cetium, (c. 334 - 262 B.C.) but it was in Seneca that the Stoics found their most eloquent advocate. Stoicism, as expressed by Seneca, helped ease pagan Rome's transition to Christianity, for it upholds ethical ideals and supports virtuous living. Stoicism also railed against the harsh treatment of slaves and the inhumane slaughter witnessed in the Roman arenas. Seneca's major contribution to a seemingly unsympathetic Stoic creed was to transform it into a powerfully moving and inspiring declaration of the dignity of the individual.

Not all people agree with the age-old ancient Greek definition of melancholy as "black bile". Some recent books argue that there are benefits to being sad. Eric Wilson's *Against Happiness: In Praise of Melancholy*, points out that melancholy: "can be a powerfully creative force (generative melancholy he terms it) that has motivated the likes of Virginia Woolf, John Keats, Vincent van Gogh and Ludwig van Beethoven[1]. He is not saying that it is "normal" or "good" to be depressed, but he is concerned that the diagnosis of any negative mood, however slight, as bad or abnormal, will lead to an eradication of one of the most powerfully inspirational and motivational forces of the human race, together with the achievements that arise from that source of motivation. Van Gogh is quoted as saying in a letter to his family: "One feels as if one were lying bound hand and foot at the bottom of a deep dark well, utterly helpless." Van Gogh is among the most famous and influential figures in the history of Western art. Unfortunately, however, his melancholy took him too far. He committed suicide at a relatively early age.

One writer that Wilson did not include, but who well could be included, is Marcel Proust. Proust's 4200 pages of anguish, sadness, and frustration over seven volumes *In Search of Lost Time* comes up with some utter miseries: "The human experience is one of anguish", he wrote, or "We must live so we can continue to suffer." Alain de Botton celebrates Proust's works, claiming that Proust can save your life.[2] His opening sentence on

Proust is "There are few things humans are more dedicated to than unhappiness". If he were talking about the untold miseries that humans have inflicted on themselves over the centuries, de Botton may be correct. In the conflicts that we see today with hundreds of thousands killed or fleeing their homelands, we will also agree with him. But de Botton is talking to us about more personal concerns: "the frailty of our bodies, the fickleness of love, the insincerities of social life, the compromises of friendship.... No event would be awaited with greater expectation than the moment of our extinction."

These are the phrases of poetry; of the romantic novel. Francis Zinmmerman provides some support to Alain de Botton as well as to Eric Wilson: the most telling expressions of depression, sadness, and melancholy, he asserts, are to be found in romance and poetry[3], "the experience of being melancholy or depressed is at the very heart of being human; feeling 'down' or blue, being dispirited, dejected, despondent, melancholy, depressed, or despairing are within the normal range. Everyone suffers from this kind of metaphorical melancholia".

Mathew Del Nevo, a philosopher at the Catholic Institute of Sydney, provides further support. In *The Valley Way of the Soul,* he writes "poets are those whose works link us singly and socially to melancholy...For real happiness we need to be in touch with our melancholy... That the good life and melancholy are linked".[4] Del Nevo also divorces melancholy from depression. Depression and morbidity, he says are "sicknesses of the soul."

Del Nevo does not give a definition of melancholy, tending to describe it in terms of its impact on people as he sees it. He includes John Keats (as did Eric Wilson) a poet of the romantic era and "considered to be among the finest in the English language".[5] Keats' short and very sad life is described by Del Nevo, who includes Keats' poem *Ode to Melancholy.*

Del Nevo also ascribes to us a soul –an attribute that we have had since time immemorial – in this as well as another of his books *The Work of Enchantment.* He suggests that it is a lack of enchantment in rich, developed countries that "causes soul-starved Westerners to experience mental (and sometimes physical) illness". This "enchantment" is most often experienced in childhood, but it also occurs in adulthood, particularly through the arts. Adults must cultivate within themselves, Del Nevo asserts, the ability to appreciate art by reading, listening, and gazing - activities often misconceived in advanced industrial societies.

Both Plato and Aristotle believed we have a soul. Virtually all religions tell us we have a soul, and that it is immortal. Plato believed that it was immortal, although Aristotle, a far more empirically based philosopher, said that it dies with us, Rene Descartes, said to be the "Father of Western Philosophy," placed our soul in the pineal gland, a small gland in the brain[6]. A good Catholic, Descartes believed in God, even making an argument – termed the Cartesian circle - for the existence of God. God, who is not a deceiver, would not allow Descartes to be mistaken about that which he clearly and distinctly perceives. Hence Descartes arrives at his well-known conclusion: "I think. Therefore, I am"

Del Nevo claims the soul is the essential us. We can perhaps translate that "us" as that inner-most set of thoughts and beliefs to which nobody else is privy, not even those closest to us. These would be the thoughts and feelings that the above writers believe is the essence of melancholy. For writers, poets, artists, sad periods, even a sad life, could produce melancholy. It could also be creative.

However, this creativity is not without its costs. For the first time, reliable data has shown that the suicide rate among people working in creative roles is significantly higher than the national average.

The first study of suicide by profession from the United Kingdom's Office for National Statistics (ONS), carried out from 2011 to 2015, showed that people who work in arts-related jobs are up to four times more likely to commit suicide.[7]

Of the many discussions on melancholy, however, the main reason for this chapter is "one of the greatest works in the English language" - *The Anatomy of Melancholy,* by Robert Burton[8]. It is to that discussion that we now turn.

The first of six editions published during the Oxford clergyman's lifetime appeared in 1621. He constantly revised it, adding his aphorisms in new editions. The reason for his book's long success is that melancholy was merely a springboard for whatever else struck the Reverend Burton's fancy. Aphorisms is perhaps not the correct description, for he labels some of his chapters as "digressions". Some are in fact, like a Russian nesting doll, digressions within digressions. I have endeavoured to repeat some of the more interesting digressions that might have some relevance to the issues of the twenty-first century, and to the findings documented in this book.

His full title is: "*The Anatomy of Melancholy. What it is: With all the Kinds, Causes, Symptomes, Prognostickes, and Several Cures of it. In Three Maine Partitions with their several Sections, Members, and Subsections. Philosophically, Medicinally, Historically, Opened and Cut Up.*"

Burton wrote it under the acronym, "Democritus Junior." Democritus was born in Greece around 460 BC and is possibly best known for his contention that atoms are the smallest part of matter. Burton probably chose this nom de plume because of Democritus's reputation – he was titled "the laughing philosopher', one who professed to tell the future and continually mocked the world's foibles. Burton's opening sentence has these characteristics: "I write of melancholy by being busy to avoid melancholy."

Some other of Burton's "digressions" include:

> "We that are bred up in learning, and, destined by our parents to this end, we suffer our childhood in the grammar-school, which .... compares it to the torments of martyrdom;

And again:

> "... when we come to the university, if we live (off) the college allowance...needy of all things but hunger and fear, or if we be maintained but partly by our parents' cost, do expend in unnecessary maintenance, books and degrees, before we come to any perfection, five hundred pounds"

> "What cannot be cured must be endured."

> "[Thou canst not think worse of me than I do of myself."

> "The tower of Babel never yielded such confusion of tongues, as the chaos of melancholy doth (in) variety of symptoms"

His definition of melancholy is "a kind of dotage without a fever, having for his ordinary companions fear and sadness, without any apparent occasion."

The Anatomy of Melancholy is available free online under Project Gutenberg.[9] His work however, is not advised as a prescription for anybody seeking to relieve their melancholy.

The above accounts of melancholy have been placed here for a second reason: to reinforce the objective of this book – the claim that the years of your old age are the best in your life. Aristotle, about 350 BC, had his versions of happiness, or flourishing. We believe that his objective, as is the objective of this book, is more acceptable to the greater number of people. But melancholy does come, to all of us, sometimes in shortish bursts, sometimes for longer periods but hopefully still transitory. As Burton describes it: "Melancholy ...goes and comes upon every small occasion of sorrow, need, sickness, trouble, fear, grief, passion, or perturbation of the mind", He adds: "from these melancholy dispositions no man living is free".

Nobody wants these occasions. Melancholy is not a benefit for us. Most of us do not want to live a life of John Keats, even if we end up as one of the finest poets of the English language. But as the following pages illustrate, there still will be, for all of us, many trade-offs to make, in seeking a happy and flourishing life.

Chapter 5

MILL, RUSSELL AND DARWIN

No great examinations of happiness - or melancholy - appeared over the subsequent centuries until the work of John Stuart Mill, along with Bertrand Russell and Charles Darwin emerged. Mill, a British philosopher and politician, set out his version of a happy life in his *Utilitarianism*, published in 1861.

We have not entirely left the Greek era, however, as Mill attributes the founding of Utilitarianism to Epicurus, a Greek philosopher who lived from 341–270 BC. Epicurus is regarded widely as a hedonist, advocating pleasure in life in preference to pain. Utility as promoted by Mill, however, is also a moral theory, which combines questions of happiness with morality.

John Stuart Mill (1806 –1873)

Mill writes[1]

> *Actions are right in proportion as they tend to promote happiness, wrong as they tend to produce the reverse of happiness. By happiness is intended pleasure, and the absence of pain; by unhappiness, pain, and the (de)privation of pleasure.*

On happiness, he writes:

> *The principal cause which makes life unsatisfactory is want of mental cultivation.... A cultivated mind ...finds sources of inexhaustible interest in all that surrounds it:*

And for sources of "inexhaustible interest", he sets out:

> *The objects of nature, the achievements of art, the imaginations of poetry, the incidents of history, the ways of mankind, past and present, and their prospects in the future.*

Sources of inexhaustible interest are allied to the findings of some of the 20th century's positive psychologists. If a personal observation may be included at this stage, however, it should be noted that all of us are different – different interests, different values. John Stuart Mill was a philosopher, a Member of Parliament and a highly-regarded contributor to human thinking. He published over 120 contributions on the betterment of society as he saw it. His thoughts on what creates happiness include the incidents of history, the ways of mankind, past and present, and their prospects in the future. They are also activities that could interest we ordinary mortals. The achievements of art and the imaginations of poetry, however, may be a little beyond the interests and inclinations of many of us.

Several of Mill's injunctions against harming others can be found in his *Utilitarianism*. The admonition that a virtuous life is desirable for happiness had already been raised by the early philosophers. When we examine the work of the positive psychologists, acting virtuously towards others is also one of their recipes for a happy life. The problem is that we cannot agree on what is virtue. In the opening paragraphs of his *Utilitarianism* Mill points out that the great thinkers of the world have disagreed on what is virtue - even on what is morality; that they have divided into different sects, and have been fighting each other since time immemorial. These conflicting moral philosophies are exclusively Western philosophies. If we search through these philosophies, which number more than twenty or so, we find three or four which are based on Mill's principle of not to harm others. It would be the most commonly occurring moral principle in the several versions of Western moral philosophy. If we search through the eastern philosophies, we find a similar injunction - Ahisma - not to harm others. It is a moral guideline that exists in the Hindu, Jain and Buddhist religions.

The Dalai Lama has expressed it as *"If you can, help others. If you can't, at least don't harm them"*.[2]

This writer first came across this injunction in the works of John Stuart Mill. It has been included under this section for that reason. To the extent that our own personal happiness is dependent on our moral behaviour, and the extent to which a government's role in ensuring our happiness can be identified are significant issues. The rule on happiness that shall be explored is a mixture of John Stuart Mill and the Dalai Lama: It is best expressed in the sentence that our moral objective in life is not to harm others, either directly or indirectly and to relieve, as best we can, the harm under which others may already be suffering.

There is little doubt that if we could collectively implement that guideline, we would increase the general level of well-being of many people in the world. It is a challenge almost impossible to fulfil, but a challenge that even the exploration of which, will increase our own satisfaction and well-being.

Bertrand Russell (1872- 1970)

Russell published *The Conquest of Happiness* in 1930, when he was just short of 60 years of age. He also emphasised the importance of cultivating interests outside oneself. To Russell, personal happiness was the best hope for ending warfare and other social ills. He did find life more worthwhile as he got older. "Now, I enjoy life; I might almost say that with every year that passes I enjoy it more". Among the factors that create a zest for life, he includes preparing and eating a good meal, affection both towards and from others, which in itself creates a sense of security, and a good family life. Finally, he included having rewarding work and the pursuit of impersonal interests.

Zest for life is a viewpoint of this book, surfacing in many ways. It was perhaps first expressed by Marcus Tullius Cicero who said when coming to the concluding chapters of his book "On Old Age."

> *To myself, indeed, the composition of this book has been so delightful, that it has not only wiped away all the disagreeableness of old age, but has even made it luxurious and delightful.*

Zest for life is also a viewpoint expressed by Epicurus, whom, the Stanford Encyclopedia of Philosophy tells us, believed he could dispense with the Platonic ideas or Forms, disprove the possibility of the soul's survival after death, and hence the prospect of punishment in the afterlife. He regarded the unacknowledged fear of death and punishment as the primary cause of anxiety among human beings, and anxiety in turn as the source of extreme and irrational desires. The elimination of the fears and corresponding desires would leave people free to pursue the pleasures, both physical and mental, to which they are naturally drawn. These are powerful beliefs.

Bertrand Russell wrote many books, most evidencing a wide concern with the issues of the world. He wrote *German Social Democracy* in 1896, in conjunction with his then wife Alys Russell; *Pragmatism* in 1909, *The Scientific Outlook*, in 1931, *History of Western Philosophy* in 1946, and *Has Man a Future* in 1961. He published *War Crimes in Vietnam* aged 95, and his autobiography in 1969, aged in his late 90s. His reasons behind his happiness then he gives as "very largely it is due to a diminishing preoccupation with myself", but also because:

"I came to centre my attention increasingly upon external objects: the state of the world, various branches of knowledge, individuals for whom I felt affection"

He includes under these external objects, financial security, work, community, friends, health, personal freedom, and moral values.

The Conquest of Happiness is a short book, available free online and worth reading. The principal lessons are encapsulated, however, in the above paragraphs.

Charles Darwin (1809-1882)

Darwin was not a philosopher. He was a biologist and the originator of the theory of evolution – a theory that has brought with it a multitude of explanations of the behaviours of the human race. Among them is our search for happiness, our moral instincts, and even war – our most destructive tendency.

Evolutionary theory, therefore, gives us a deeper understanding of ourselves, and with that understanding a greater capability in identifying those behaviours that will provide a greater satisfaction with life. Peter Crabb, a psychologist, reinforces this opinion in a review of Bjorn Grinde's book on Darwinian Happiness[3]. He states:

"If we can grasp how our brains and behaviour work, then surely we can alter our behaviour and the course of history."[4]

Charles Darwin's best-known works are *On the Origin of the Species by Means of Natural Selection* (1859); *The Descent of Man, and Selection in Relation to Sex* (1871), followed by *The Expression of the Emotions in Man and Animals* (1872). Although the work of a biologist, they are in the tradition of empirical philosophy, that of Aristotle, for they cast an increasing light on human nature. Much of this exploration of human nature was opened by Darwin, but it has raised questions which are still being unravelled today.

Darwin, on war and on human cooperation, for instance, has given us one of the most insightful of observations in the English language:

It must not be forgotten that although a high standard of morality gives but a slight advantage or no advantage to each individual man and his children over the other men of the same tribe . . . [t]here can be no doubt that a tribe including many members who, from pos-

sessing in a high degree the spirit of patriotism, fidelity, obedience, courage, and sympathy, were always ready to aid one another, and to sacrifice themselves for the common good, would be victorious over most other tribes; and this would be natural selection.

He states in *Origin of Species,* however, that "forms that are successful in the struggle for existence are deemed to be slightly better adapted than those with which they have had to compete for their places in the economy of nature".

In other words, Darwin described human existence as a struggle. Elsewhere he notes that the tribe that aids one another may be more successful in the "competition for resources". It is reasonable to assume that this competition lies behind most wars. The tribe that saw that the adjacent river valley offered larger and more reliable food supply, even if occupied by another tribe, if it attacked and took over that land, would be the more successful tribe.

Darwin also thought that happiness lay in marriage – a theory that has been given much support in the responses to those surveyed for this book. He scribbled on a letter from a friend a carefully considered list of pros ("constant companion," "charms of music & female chit-chat") and cons ("means limited," "no books," "terrible loss of time") regarding marriage and its potential impact on his work.[5] The list is found in the Correspondence of Charles Darwin,

Just a few days before his marriage to Emma Wedgwood in 1839, he wrote:

My own dearest Emma, I earnestly pray, you may never regret the great, & I will add very good, deed, you are to perform on the Tuesday: My own dear future wife, God bless you.

Darwin was married to his first cousin. They had 10 children, but three died before age 10, two from infectious diseases. Three of the six surviving children with long-term marriages did not produce any offspring. His children were the grandchildren of Josiah Wedgwood, founder of Wedgewood Pottery. Emma was Wedgewood's daughter. A prominent abolitionist, Wedgwood is also remembered for his anti-slavery medallion engraved with "Am I Not a Man and a Brother?". Josiah Wedgwood sent a packet of his medallions to Benjamin Franklin, then president of the Pennsylvania Society for the Abolition of Slavery. Britain's Committee to Abolish the Slave Trade also adopted this phrase.

In 1861 Emma wrote to Darwin, then plagued by accusations that he was committing heresy: "I feel in my inmost heart your admirable qualities & feelings & all I would hope is that you might direct them upwards."

Emma's and his own inheritances enabled Darwin to support his research in natural history. One of the findings from the questionnaire to the over 65s outlined later in this study is that at least a 'comfortable' income is necessary for happiness. We may not need to be wealthy, but it does enable us to fulfil many of the objectives identified in the responses to the survey.

Charles and Emma Darwin did work together. Scientific American in its May 24, 2010 edition tells us that the research notes and tables filled with the illegible scrawl of Darwin's elderly hands and the neater writing of his wife Emma eventually resulted in the 1872 publication of *The Expression of the Emotions in Man and Animals*. Here he argued that all humans and other animals, show emotion through remarkably similar behaviours.

Chapter 6

THE MODERN RESEARCHERS

The last half century or more has seen a massive increase in research on ageing, along with, in more recent times, the growth of a new science – positive psychology. They are closely interlinked: the first group of studies attempts to find out what makes us age, and the second attempts to determine what makes us happy. It has been found that when we are happy, or well-satisfied with our lives, we live longer. This chapter attempts to identify the factors at work in both cases.

Ageing studies

Begun in 1938, the Harvard aging study is the oldest, most thorough study of ageing yet undertaken. The study consisted of three stages: a sample of 268 socially advantaged Harvard graduates born about 1920; a second stage of 456 socially disadvantaged inner-city men born about 1930; and a third sample of 90 middle-class, intellectually gifted women born about 1910. One of the principal investigators was George Vaillant, who has documented the results in his book *Aging Well* [1]. Valliant writes: "It is social aptitude, not intellectual brilliance or parental social class that leads to successful aging." Robert Waldinger, a psychiatrist at Massachusetts General Hospital and a professor of psychiatry at Harvard Medical School, is currently the director of the study. In a recent TED talk, he stated that there were three factors that contributed to happiness: 1. Close relationships, 2. The quality of these relationships, and 3. Stable supportive marriages.

John F. Kennedy was a participant in the Harvard graduate component. At the time of writing, only 19 were still alive, all aged in their 90s.

The Harvard study found that there are six factors at age 50 that have a great deal to do with whether you will get to age 80:

1. a warm marriage,
2. possessing adaptive or coping strategies,

3. not smoking heavily,
4. not abusing alcohol,
5. getting ample exercise and
6. not being overweight.

One 84-year-old study member answered: "I live to work, to learn something that I didn't know yesterday, and to enjoy the precious moments with my wife."

Waldinger reinforces the contribution of a good marriage: "It was how satisfied they were in their relationships. The people who were the most satisfied in their relationships at age 50 were the healthiest at age 80." In a recent component of the study, researchers found that women who felt securely attached to their partners were less depressed and happier in their relationships and also had better memory functions than those with frequent marital conflicts. A full description of the findings of this study can be found on the Science Blog under 'Good Genes are Nice'.[2]

Another study is The Oxford [Ohio] Ageing Study. In 1975 gerontologist Robert Atchley contacted every resident over the age of 50 in the town of Oxford, Ohio. About two-thirds of those contacted - over 1,100 people - agreed to participate in Atchley's study. Becca Levy followed up on the study and published her findings in the Journal of Gerontology in 2003.[3] The follow-up studies were sponsored by the American Psychological Association. The broad findings were:

- People with more positive views of their own aging lived, on average, 7.6 years longer than people with more negative views.
- Participants' will to live - as measured by descriptions of their lives as hopeful or hopeless, worthless or worthy, as empty or full - correlated with both their perceptions of aging and their lifespan.
- People who don't dwell on the negative changes that come with age generally seem to do best.
- The most cheerful children died earlier, possibly caused by a more careless attitude toward their health - they were somewhat more likely to drink, smoke and take other risks.
- Seniors who held negative self-stereotypes about aging tended to lose more of their hearing over the course of three years than seniors with more positive views of ageing.

The United States does not hold the monopoly on ageing studies. The Cambridge University Well-being Institute also published a study, *Flour-*

ishing across Europe, by Felicia Huppert & Timothy So, covering 40,000 people in 23 countries.[4] It measured ten features of positive well-being. These features combine "hedonic and eudaimonic aspects of well-being: competence, emotional stability, engagement, meaning, optimism, positive emotion, positive relationships, resilience, self-esteem, and vitality".

Note that Huppert and So revert to Aristotle's word eudaimonia to describe well-being. The study revealed a four-fold difference in flourishing rates across countries, from 41% of the population in Denmark having positive views on their well-being to less than 10% in Slovakia, Russia and Portugal. There are also striking differences in country profiles across the 10 well-being features.

An Australian study on ageing conducted by the Flinders University Centre for Ageing Studies came up with roughly similar results. It tracked 2087 participants aged 65 years or more from 1992 to the final data collection in 2014

Key findings (primarily using the study's own words) were:[5]

- Social networks comprising discretionary relationships were protective against mortality.
- Depressive symptoms present a greater risk for mortality for men than for women.
- Factors including intact cognitive functioning, higher expectancy of control over life, and for women, better morale, were linked to better survival odds over 8 years, independent of health and physical functioning.
- Medical conditions that were reported most frequently at the first set of interviews were arthritis, hypertension, skin cancer, corns and bunions and cataracts. For the most part, these continued over the period of the study.
- Risk factors for mortality included under-nutrition and lack of exercise:
- Risk factors for depression are starting the study as a widow, being in, or moving to, a residential aged care facility, and experiencing difficulties in the activities of daily living. Two-thirds to three-quarters of participants showed no signs of depression.

The report concludes that strategies that encourage regular exercise, supportive social networks and that engender a positive emotional state of mind help promote survival and a good quality of life for older Australians.

The United Nations have also produced happiness reports

In 2012, the UN started publishing an annual World Happiness Report - a survey of the state of global happiness that ranks 155 countries on six key indicators: freedom, generosity, health, social support, income, and trustworthy governance. By these measures, Norway, Denmark, and Iceland took the top spots in 2017. The US came 14th.

The OECD[6] has also produced a number of reports, the first in 2001 by the Centre for Educational Research and Innovation: The Well-being of Nations. *The Role of Human and Social Capital. This* report points out the economic benefits of developing the human capital of a country – the educational skills and accomplishments of the people of the country. It also argues that with increased educational levels comes increased happiness and well-being. In 2013 it produced *The OECD guidelines on measuring subjective well-being*[7],and in 2015, *In it together: Why less inequality benefits all.*[8] In the 2013 book, the OECD measured eleven facets of wellbeing ranging across incomes, jobs, health, skills, and housing to civic engagement and learning

The 2015 book emphasizes the growing gap between the rich and the poor and the increasing ownership of the world's wealth by a smaller and smaller percentage of individuals. It argues that these trends militate against overall economic growth. It may be a trend that an observer would wish to see corrected, but will have an impact on happiness and wellbeing only for the very poorest.

The Positive Psychologists

Positive psychology is a new science, founded in 1998 by Martin Seligman. The Positive Psychology Institute will tell you that it is the scientific study of human flourishing, an applied approach to optimal functioning. It has also been defined as the study of the strengths and virtues that enable individuals, communities and organisations to thrive.

There are five founding fathers to the discipline: William James, Abraham Maslow, Martin Seligman, Mihaly Czikszentmihalyi and Christopher Peterson. The first is a philosopher/scientist who set the stage; the last four are psychologists. William James (1842-1910) was a leading philosopher and a medical doctor. He and Charles Sanders Peirce founded the school of philosophical pragmatism. He graduated from the Harvard Medical School in 1869, writing *Principles of Psychology* in 1890. For James, happiness is a result of our being active participants in the game of life. He writes, "Believe that life is worth living, and your very belief will help create the fact."[9]

Abraham Maslow is the psychologist responsible for the oft-quoted hierarchy of human needs, expressed in his 1954 book *Motivation and Personality*. These needs are self-actualisation, esteem, love & belonging, safety, and physiological needs. The last- mentioned are physical needs such as air, water, food, clothing and shelter, required by all humans. The relevance of Maslow's hierarchy will become relevant as we dig further into the research findings of the positive psychologists.

Martin Seligman, Mihaly Czikszentmihalyi and Christopher Peterson are positive psychologists and it is to their work, and that of several others, that we now turn.

Martin Seligman: Elected President of the American Psychological Association in 1998 Seligman founded positive psychology as a distinct scientific discipline. He is Professor of Psychology and director of the Positive Psychology Center at the University of Pennsylvania. Author of over 20 books, the three-best known of which are *Learned Optimism*. (1990), *Authentic Happiness: Using the New Positive Psychology to Realize Your Potential for Lasting Fulfilment*. (2002), and *Flourish, A visionary new understanding of happiness and well-being* (2011). Seligman argues that the goal is well-being, not happiness. and that it has five constituents:

- **Positive Emotion**: We feel pleasure, rapture, ecstasy, warmth, comfort, etc. We are happy; satisfied with life; we 'feel good.'
- **Engagement**: We are 'hooked into' what we are doing, absorbed by it. We lose track of time.
- **Relationships:** We relate well with other people - friends, our partner, even to doing good deeds for strangers.
- **Meaning**: We belong to and serve something bigger than ourselves - often pursued for its own sake.
- **Achievement**: The extent to which we achieve our goals. It is a product of the skill we have and the effort we put in.

This gives us the acronym PERMA. Each of the constituents is measurable – we can 'feel good' but we can also measure it. Positive emotion is the 'yes' response in the questionnaire that was sent out to people over 65 as part of this study. The findings from this questionnaire are documented in the next chapter of this book.

Christopher Peterson. Professor of Psychology at the University of Michigan, Peterson researched and wrote with Martin Seligman *Character Strengths and Virtues: A Handbook and Classification*. It is a powerful listing of twenty-four personal strengths which lead to a fulfilling life. The list, shown in Figure 6.1, is a modern research-based statement that in a sense, updates Aristotle's 12 virtues. It was published by the American Psychological Association in 2004.

Figure 6.1
Character Strengths & Virtues

STRENGTHS OF WISDOM AND KNOWLEDGE:

1. Creativity

2. Curiosity

3. Open-mind

4. Love of learning

5. Perspective [wisdom]:

STRENGTHS OF COURAGE:

6. Bravery [but not limited to physical bravery]:

7. Persistence [perseverance, industriousness]:

8. Integrity [authenticity, honesty]:

9. Vitality [zest, enthusiasm, vigour, energy]:

STRENGTHS OF HUMANITY:

10. Love

11. Kindness

12. Social intelligence

INTERPERSONAL STRENGTHS:

13. Teamwork

14. Treating all people the same, with fairness and justice

15. Leadership

VIRTUES OF TEMPERANCE:

16. Forgiveness and mercy

17. Humility and modesty

18. Prudence

19. Self-Regulation and Self-control

TRANSCENDANCE:

20. Appreciation of Beauty and Excellence

21. Gratitude

22. Hope

23. Humour

24. Spirituality

Source: Christopher Peterson, (2004). Character Strengths and Virtues. A Handbook and Classification. American Psychological Association.

Peterson has also published *A Primer in Positive Psychology* (2006)

Mihaly Csikszentmihalyi Seligman and Csikszentmihalyi cooperated on a 2014 book *Positive Psychology: An Introduction*. Csíkszentmihalyi, Hungarian born and former head of the Department of Psychology at the University of Chicago is, however, perhaps best known for his book *Flow*. He describes flow as "being completely involved in an activity for its own sake. The ego falls away. Time flies. Every action, movement, and thought follows inevitably from the previous one, like playing jazz. Your whole being is involved, and you're using your skills to the utmost". He adds:

> *Each of us is born with two contradictory sets of instructions: a conservative tendency made up of instincts for self-preservation, self-aggrandizement, and saving in energy, and an expansive tendency made up of instincts for exploring, for enjoying novelty and risk. We need both.*

Corey Keyes and Jonathan Haidt These two psychologists edited *Flourishing: Positive Psychology and the Life Well-Lived*, published by the American Psychological association in 2003. Three main findings on worthwhile activities stand out in their study of the good life:

- a sense of meaning and a richness emerge in life as people immerse themselves in activities and relationships,
- the pursuit of intrinsically satisfying goals like overcoming adversity, and
- serving one's community through volunteering, and other fulfilling activities.

That book sets out the analyses used to study the good life, expanding the scope of social and psychological research to include happiness, well-being, courage, citizenship, play, and the satisfactions of healthy work and healthy relationships. Martin Seligman provided a foreword to the book on the past and future of positive psychology.

The next few paragraphs will set out the theories espoused by three additional positive psychologists, Todd Kashdan, Richard Layard and Paul Martin (the last two together) before documenting in the next chapter the findings from the paper's research questionnaire.

Todd Kashdan, Professor of Psychology at George Mason University, Kashdan works on well-being, social anxiety, anxiety disorder, positive psychology, and emotion regulation. His books include *The Upside of Your Dark Side: Why being your whole self - not just your good self - drives success and fulfilment* (2014); *Mindfulness, Acceptance, and Positive Psychology: The Seven Foundations of Well-Being* (2013); *Designing Positive Psychology: Taking Stock and Moving Forward - Series in Positive Psychology* (2011); Curious? *Discover the Missing Ingredient to a Fulfilling Life* (2010). Attempting to summarise Kashdan's thoughts on a flourishing life is a daunting task, but a reasonable answer might include:

- Being curious.
- Being open to new experiences.
- Being able to effectively manage ambiguity and uncertainty.
- Being able to adapt to the demands required of different situations (what his editor termed "psychological flexibility").
- Discovering our strengths, deepest values, and what it is we are passionate about.
- Strengthening connections to these values and passionate pursuits so that we can pursue a life aligned with them.

Richard Layard and Paul Martin These two researchers canvassed countless surveys and scientific tests to reach similar general conclusions. They are documented in *Happiness: Lessons from a New Science* by Richard Layard[10], and Paul Martin's *Making Happy People: The nature of happiness and its origins in childhood.* [11] Their findings on avoiding an unhappy life are summarised below:

- the emotional ties of family,
- financial security,
- work,
- community,
- friends,
- health,
- personal freedom, and
- moral values.

They add that our aim as a society should be to increase happiness, as opposed to increasing income and GDP as ends in themselves. In that the collective decisions of our societies are made by our elected representatives, it is not a massive leap to assert that one role of government is to ensure, as far as it can, the happiness and wellbeing of its people. Cicero's belief that our moral duty is to promote the well-being of our fellow citizens gives support to this contention.[12] Cicero may only be providing us with an individual moral guideline, but for us all, he does, as do Richard Layard and Paul Martin, provide a moral rule for our government. How a government fulfils that obligation is not a simple decision as will be explored in subsequent pages.

Layard, who is Baron Layard, program director of the Centre for Economic Performance at the London School of Economics, supports Aristotle's call on virtue. A review by William Davies of the Institute for Policy research, agrees, pointing out that Layard argues: "The decline of orthodox Christianity and then of social solidarity has left a moral vacuum... The social facts which cause us unhappiness – divorce, loneliness, crime – tend mostly to be symptoms of moral deficiency. Meanwhile, happiness increases in circumstances where we become locked into circumstances of trust and cooperation."[13] Davies states that Layard is echoing Emile Durkheim. He also describes Layard's work as being "a fiercely moralistic book."

Ed Diener and others. Diener, professor of psychology at the University of Illinois, either alone or with others, has written several books and research papers on well-being.[14] If we attempt to summarise his main findings on what contributes to well-being, they are:

- Purpose in life
- Positive relationships
- Competence
- Self-esteem
- Optimism
- Contribution to the well-being of others.

Diener uses the concept "hedonic psychology", stating that there are both pleasures of the mind and pleasures of the body. He differentiates between the two. This author accepts that there are two distinct sets of pleasures, and that pleasures of the mind and of the senses do describe them. Those of the mind are perhaps encapsulated effectively in the term curiosity. Of all these prescriptions, the author would favour Tod Kashdan's, of which being curious, open to new experiences, and pursuing our deepest passions would be prime recommendations.

Note that Diener and his companions include the attribute "self-esteem" which could be considered somewhat similar to Seligman's "Achievement".

Barbara Fredrickson. Kenan Distinguished Professor of Psychology at the University of North Carolina, Barbara Fredrickson has given us an answer to the problem of what we do when we are down. How do we encourage a positive feeling? In her book *Positivity* she talks about nourishing power of small, positive moments of accumulating "micro-moments of positivity," We need to get essential daily nutrients—not only from food, but also from a laugh, a hug or even a smaller moment of positive emotion, especially with someone with whom we engage readily. In 2013 Fredrickson released *Love 2.0. Finding Happiness and Health in Moments of Connection.* The book serves as a guide to learn how to increase opportunities to receive and provide moments of love. Fredrickson describes love, as being an emotion that, like all emotions, is momentary, not enduring and can be experienced in micro-moments. Love, through this lens, is not an emotion for just soul mates and/or family ties. Love 2.0 defines love as an emotion that can be shared several times a day with different people ranging from family members to strangers on the street.

Frederickson's thoughts as expressed in her Book Love 2.0 are very convincing.

Summarising the positive psychologists

Several common themes come through in the findings of today's psychological researchers. The differences appear to be minor, and primarily a matter of emphasis

The most common themes are versions of Seligman's Engagement and Meaning: We are 'hooked into' what we are doing, absorbed by it. We lose track of time that we belong to and serving something bigger than ourselves.

Also, up there are relationships, with family, friends, and your partner. This finding is confirmed by the responses to the author's questionnaire.

Mentioned, but not by all researchers, are curiosity, and positive emotion. Curiosity is rated highly because it signifies an enquiring mind, a mind that asks questions and searches for answers. Those answers may lead to activities that are in themselves, totally satisfying and enjoyable. This writer accepts both, but possibly for slightly different reasons than the psychologists. They are discussed, along with some differences, under personal reflections in Chapter 9.

Finally, there is virtue as altruism, mentioned in several different ways – helping others, promoting their well-being, or volunteering. The concept of virtue as a path to happiness may at first seem odd to a modern observer, but as we explore the findings of the various researchers, and the responses to the surveys, we find that virtue, specifically defined, does have a positive contribution to make to our lives.

Chapter 7

THE FINDINGS OF THE SURVEY

The questionnaire, sent out to every person aged over 65 that I could locate, is set out in Figure 7.1. 155 responses were received. The overall results were 87 YES, life after 65 is happier, to 68 NO answers. The respondents supplied their own answers to the question of why they were or were not happier now than when they were younger. The reasons for answering a Yes or No are the author's interpretations and categorisation of those answers. The results are tabled below in Figures 7.2 & 7.3

For the most part, categorising the answers under the headings in Figures 7.2 and 7.3 was relatively straightforward. A few answers were difficult to categorise. This classification difficulty affected the NO answers primarily, in the responses to why people felt their early years were better. Earlier years more fulfilling (28) or earlier years more financially rewarding (7) was an attempt to unravel answers that stated in various unclear ways that a respondent's earlier years were, in fact, more personally fulfilling or financially rewarding. It does appear that for a person who was a high achiever during their working life, the comedown to an ordinary life, possibly on a retirement pension was just that – a comedown. Those beyond 65 who answered no for this reason may, of course, be quite satisfied with their lives now. Just that they consider their lives before 65 more satisfying.

One change made early in the enquiry was to allow for people who could not decide between their happiness in life before or after 65. It was initially thought that everybody could make this decision, but it became increasingly obvious that some people just could not decide. Provision had to be made in the questionnaire to allow for this possibility. At times, the "Could not decide" vote was quite high. The result for an inquiry at a Sydney based Probus club for instance, with 46 respondents, shows the undecided at just under 20%:

Number of YESs: 18; Number of NOs: 18; Could not decide: 10

A note on the records made for this survey states, incidentally, that it was the: "First dead heat of YESs and NOs in a dozen surveys" Overall, for the study, the could-not-decides were about 25. The figure is inexact as the option was not available in the first few surveys.

Figure 7.1
Questionnaire

Name…   **(First name or alias); Age   years; M or F?**

Some people argue that your post retirement years (65+) are the best years of your life. They give many reasons: greater freedom enables you to do anything you want; they have found an activity(ies), which are very fulfilling. Others argue no, that declining health, lack of money, closeness to death, make life less than totally happy. Or perhaps greater achievements earlier in life outweigh those now.

Do you agree, ON BALANCE, that 65+ are the best years of your life? (Cross against one)

- YES

or

- NO

- Why did you give that answer? [You can give a "Cannot Decide" answer (with reasons), if you cannot <u>really</u> decide].

Have you found a special interest(s)? What is it? Are they? Enough for a 'YES, DEFINITELY'?

- Born where?
- Live where/at home?   Retirement community?
- Household income
  Bottom. 0 … Average 5 ….. Top percentile 10
- Where did you learn of this survey?

Reply by email to peterbowden@ozemail.com.au

Or post to Dr. Peter Bowden, Department of Philosophy, University of Sydney, Sydney, NSW, 2006.

THANK YOU

THE FINDINGS OF THE SURVEY 51

The possibility does exist that the predominance of YES over NO for an answer reflected the fact that the respondent was still alive and enjoying life. The respondent could have given a YES for this reason. This thinking may possibly have influenced some answers, but it is believed that this influence is relatively small. The question was clear and specific, and, with the wisdom that is supposed to come with age, would have been well understood. In addition, in the discussions that followed many of the surveys, although a number expressed their joy in life (along with a number who expressed the opposite), it was clear that the main survey question was fully understood.

One weakness of the survey is that it did not capture cross-section of society. The survey was not deliberately directed at people who had higher levels of education, and therefore likely to be better off, but the methods used to gather the information would have had that effect. One workshop was conducted in a retirement home, but the results of that survey gave the same answers as the overall survey – people preferred life after 65 to life before. Also, the survey results that show satisfaction with life increases with age, also tends to show that the conventional wisdom – unhappiness with life depends on wealth; also that it increases as one gets older and less firm. However, extensions of this research, which are in the pipeline, will be shown on the book's website

The other point to mention is that the response rate was appalling. The surveys sent out through seniors' organisations via email went out as a request to respond to the actual questionnaire developed by a researcher examining happiness in old age achieved a very low response rate. At times, the response was a little over one percent of the people to whom the email survey was sent. The reason is unclear, but it is thought that the use of email to gather the responses did not appeal to the over 65s. That email requesting that people fill in the survey provided the results that had been achieved from the surveys that had been completed to that point. It was thought that providing participants with the results that had been achieved to that point in time would encourage a response. These steps did not appear to lift the response rate to any noticeable degree. In addition, respondents at workshops received an immediate feedback on their results.

The YES Answers

The reasons behind providing a YES answer are set out in Figure 7.2. By far the overriding reason was freedom to do whatever you wanted to do with your time. This response is obviously the major benefit behind retiring from a working life. As one respondent reported, you are free to get up in the morning, and work assiduously at your chosen activities. Alternately, you are free to spend the morning over breakfast with the newspaper, or even free to go back to bed.

The remaining list of responses also informs us about what people did with that freedom. Top of the list was travel, next was learning, curiosity, then leisure, spelled out in a variety of smaller ways, along with financial security. The relatively high place of financial security on the listing corresponded with Aristotle's injunction 2500 years earlier, that you need to have sufficient of the world's goods to enjoy a eudaimistic life.

Travel is the odd man out in comparison with the philosophers and psychologists. Neither of these two research categories mention travel. The fact that travel is not mentioned by these other sources is, however, unlikely to be an aberration. The ancient philosophers travelled widely, often using the observations from their travels for their learning and writing. Aristotle, we know, lived in at least four different countries, and travelled to many more for his investigations into political systems

Travel for many people, even for those of a far less inquiring mind than Aristotle, has many benefits. One is that it is a learning exercise. We visit nature's beauties, and marvel. Or ancient places of great history and learn that history. We question why nations so much poorer than we are today, could build such magnificent buildings – cathedrals, mosques, even multi-arched bridges. The aqueducts of the Roman empire still make us marvel. Or we visit places of torture, and again wonder why? Places where they tortured people for holding very Christian beliefs that were deemed heretical at that time. What were they hoping to achieve?

Will Ruger of the Charles Koch Institute, a philanthropic organization encouraging discussion on topics like free speech, foreign policy, and criminal justice reform:

> *"Foreign travel provides a lot of benefits, including getting to better understand other cultures. But it also allows one to better appreciate that despite all of the ways that the world is "smaller" and more interconnected today, the world is still a big place,*

The chapter on personal thoughts details some discussions with some respondents that ranked travel highly. Their responses were consistently couched in terms of exciting and interesting new adventures.

Figure 7.2
Reasons Behind Yes Answers

- Freedom to do whatever   42
- Travel   27
- Learning, curiosity   21
- Self-acceptance   13
- Close partner   12
- Less stress   6
- Wiser   4
- Grandchildren   14
- Volunteering /helping others 11
- Financial Security   19
- Personal achievement   10
- Good friends   18
- Music   13
- Leisure   19

Learning, curiosity is third on the list of rankings, a finding that collaborates well with the modern psychologists, and to some extent, with the reasons why some people enjoy a longer life. Unfortunately, the research answers rarely informed us what were the major items on the learning list. Some speculative thoughts, based on the answers and the discussions that followed the questionnaire, are provided in later chapters.

Note also that good friends are high on the ranking, an answer that supports the evidence for the inclusion of friendships as a historically consistent factor in contributing to peoples' well-being for over 2000 years.

Most of these answers would be applicable whether you were older than 65 or younger. One answer that should be pointed out that would appear to be tied to being older, was your personal acceptance of the vagaries and difficulties of life. Several responders gave the answer – self-acceptance, an answer that signified, in various ways, that they no longer were concerned with what people thought about them; that they were happy with themselves. It seemed to this observer a heart-warming way in which to reach your final years. Although, we must remember what Aristotle said over 2000 years earlier. Old people, he said "are not shy"; that they "neither love warmly nor hate bitterly". These are issues worthy of further exploration.

The NO Answers

The overriding answer by people who had responded NO to the question whether the years after 65 were the best of their lives. Set out in Figure 7, it was that the earlier years were either more fulfilling, or more financially rewarding. The responses were worded in several different ways which were not always clearly classifiable in either of these two categories. In the group discussions that often followed these surveys, it became apparent that those who supplied either of these for a NO answer, who were almost always male, had held a relatively high-level job – and that he now regarded his present occupation – that of a retired person -as warranting a NO answer.

Figure 7.3
Reasons Behind No Answers

•	Earlier years more fulfilling	22
•	Earlier years more financially rewarding	6
•	Ill Health today	15
•	Death - friends/ relatives	10
•	65+ years less fulfilling	2
•	Lack of purpose	2
•	Poverty, or nearly so	1
•	Loss of sex drive	1
•	Carer for family	2
•	Shortage of likeminded people	1
•	No zest for life	3

They may have answered with a NO, but it is doubtful that any of these respondents are depressed. It does seem disappointing, however, to find a man (it was always a man) who has been successful, being unwilling to use whatever capabilities he may have to take up a new and engrossing activity or project in his retired years This writer also received the distinct impression during some of the conversations that respondents who set out this answer tended to be of a politically conservative inclination. The number of people responding does not equate to the number of responses as some responses were garbled, and difficult to classify.

Ill-health today was the next highest on the list. This was expected to be, and so turned out as factual, as the major reason why older people are less than happy.

This would be an expected outcome of the increased lifespans that have developed over the years. Many health conditions and associated impairments, such as arthritis, dementia, and hearing loss, become more common as people get older. John, 83, was a NO. He wrote "A near death experience at the age of 66 meant that I could no longer play tennis, a game of which I was very fond; and I had to give up travel. My intellectual capability was unimpaired, and this was some compensation". Bernice, 75, who could have been an undecided, but voted for a NO, wrote: "Negatives are health, problems of living in a retirement home. My mother died 3 years ago. I miss her greatly. Positives are that I still paint and have several really good friends".

We can expect such an answer from older people, but it also sent this research off in the direction of determining what makes for a longer and healthier life. To summarise those findings, however, we need only to quote Cicero, who said 2000 years ago that we should eat well and take adequate exercise.

One finding that appeared at odds with normal expectations is that the number of people who preferred life after to life before 65 increased with the age of the respondent. One would normally expect as additional aches and pains come with age, the preference for life after 65 would fall off. In fact, it increased for males, as shown in Figure 7.4. And was essentially the same for females.

Figure 7.4
Average age of YES and NO responders

AVERAGE AGE OF A SAMPLE of YES:

| 33 MALES | 74.2 years |
| 29 FEMALES | 73.4 years |

Average Age of a Sample of NOs:

| 19 MALES | 72.1 years |
| 20 FEMALES | 73.5 years |

[Not all responses supplied age]

As a contribution to the group discussions held after the surveys, the author prepared a list of people who had continued to be successful after reaching 65. This list, The Golden Oldies, is shown in Figure 7.5. The list is principally of people who continue to be successful in their chosen field after they turn 65. But that does not negate the assertion that a person who has been successful in one field cannot contribute in another field.

Figure 7.5
The Golden Oldies

	Born	
Harrison Ford	1942	Injured in crash landing of own plane at Santa Monica Ca.
Nana Mouskouri	1934	Campaigns for Australia to release asylum seeker children.
James Patterson	1947	Has sold more than 300 million books. First person to sell 1 million e-books
Sigourney Weaver	1949	New movie *Avatar 2*.
Helen Mirren	1945	*Eye in the Sky*, Currently filming *The Good Liar*
Richie Benaud	1930	Sports announcer. Last public engagement 2014 died that year
Christie Brinkley	1954	Appeared in a turquoise swimming costume on the cover of People magazine. Magazines have named Brinkley one of the most attractive women of all time.
Tom Keneally	1935	Latest book Crimes of the Father 2016
Honor Blackman	1925	Played Pussy Galore in a 007 movie. On stage in 2007, Still active
Cyril Baldock	1940	Swam English Channel 2014. First time at 40.
Dorothy Rowe	1930	Psychologist writer on depression, still giving public talks
Harriet Thompson	1923	Running marathons into her 90's. Died at 94
Inge Syllm-Rapoport	1913	Presented with her PhD by Hamburg University in 2015
Vera Lynn	1917	On March 20th 2017. Will shortly release a new album
Diana Rigg	1938	The Queen of Thorns in Game of Thrones, Rigg is best known for her role as the only Mrs. James Bond.
Robert Mugabe	1924	Recently ousted President of Zimbabwe (but not "golden").

Death of friends or relative is next on the list. The average age of death in the United States in 2012 was 78.8 years. With the average age of the respondents being about 74 years, it is inevitable that almost all people of that age will have experienced the death of their parents and will know a friend or acquaintance or even partner that will have died. Sometimes the wrench is quite dramatic.

Widows

An off-the-cuff assessment would consider widowhood extremely difficult to accept. Searching through the literature on widowhood, together with many of the answers to the questionnaire, indicates that loneliness is the greatest problem following the loss of a spouse. But very few questionnaire responses placed becoming a widow an issue of some impact. And the answers provided a variety of results. One respondent was completely distraught by the "loss of my closest friend in life after near on fifty years". Another, although recording a warm and loving marriage of some forty years, and saddened by the loss of her partner, nevertheless felt liberated. The marriage was one where he made the decisions, but now she was undertaking the activities that she herself desired.

Renata Singer, wife of Peter Singer, the Ira W. Decamp Professor of Bioethics at Princeton University, interviewed 28 women aged between 85 and 100 during 2012 and 2013. *Older & Bolder. Life after 60*, documents her findings.[1] She demonstrates how the last third of a woman's life can be productive and full of joy. Women tend to outlive their partners. What is less predictable is how they cope with being alone in the world after so many years of companionship.

The women that Renata Singer interviewed were from varying backgrounds and different economic circumstances. A July18, 2015 article in the Sydney Morning Herald "Do you miss me tonight?" written by Singer, describes her findings from 20 widows from Australia and the United States. Their responses varied enormously. The responses from this writer's discussions also show great variation:

"It happens, you have to face it"; "I believe we will meet in the afterlife"; I really lost him with Alzheimer's;" "We had a horrible life. He drank;"; "I have everything I need", "He lead me to a miserable life", "Loneliness is the biggest issue" were among the answers recorded in the discussions.

There is no one overall finding that one can make on widowhood. Each person is free to make her own choices on a path towards renewed fulfillment and life satisfaction.

It should be mentioned that the loss of a spouse was not mentioned by any male respondents. That women do live longer than men may be one reason, but it would seem that the loss of a spouse would equally affect both sexes

The writer will also mention a small survey undertaken on a cruise boat in France, on the Gironde, near Bordeaux. There were 130 people on the boat, not all of whom were over 65. The purser, however, told us that the age applied to most people on that boat and to most boats on the same excursion. We received 13 answers to a translated version of the questionnaire. An analysis of these answers shows that six were yes, eight were no, and two were unable to decide. The French reasons for their answers were

The reasons for yes answers

1. Fewer daily obligations
2. Free time (two answers)
3. Having projects that were interesting and the time to work on them
4. Good health
5. Still working and successful
6. Divorced and happy with being so

The reasons for the no answers

1. You lose your physical capabilities, (Two answers)
2. You will soon lose your intellectual capabilities
3. You lose your autonomy even though you have enough time to do things that you like
4. Lack of energy in making too many touring trips
5. Becoming a widow (two answers)
6. Being divorced at 60 years of age

Two people could not decide. The reasons given were that life is good both before and after. It is not possible to extend this survey to all of France for the sample is too small. Of note for this paragraph, is the response to widowhood was also a stronger negative than the earlier Australian results.

The findings on the boat in Bordeaux are somewhat counteracted by an article in Le Figaro in March 2018 *You feel younger than your age? It is a positive sign.*[2] The article first quotes a US study that questioned 500,000 people aged 10 to 89. Most people feel that they are ten years less than their actual age. This remains true up to around 80 years of age, when the ten-year gap lessens. The article, however, does not rely solely on US sources, quoting French and Danish studies on old age. The Danish study of nearly 1,500 Danes by David Rubin of Duke University, North Carolina and Dorthe Berntsen of the University of Aarhus in Denmark found similar results except that in Denmark, the older we got the gap widened between the age felt and the actual age.

Gilles Berrut, Professor of Geriatric Medicine and fondateur du Gérontopôle des Pays de la Loire et Serge, in his book on ageing reported that

27% of the responders of more than 40 years had a perceived age which corresponded well to their real age and that only 2% felt older than their age.[3] He also stated "There is a kind of double picture. We meet every day people between 70 and 80 years old. They are fully autonomous, very active, with a pleasant life overall; yet, when we talk about older people, it's all about their problems, never about what's right." In other words, older people talk about their problems. Also, as stated by the deputy mayor of Le Havre in charge of health, the elderly and disability, Valérie Egloff, at the 2017 Health Communication Festival last November: "Aging is not a curse, but the good news is that we are still alive."

Friends

Friendship is high on the positive answers. Dale Carnegie's book *How to win friends and influence people* has been constantly in print since it was first published in 1936. It is not entirely clear that Carnegie's recommendations on friendships are the types of friendships mentioned in the survey results. Or in the psychological literature. Carnegie presented six points. In the discussions on the responses that followed the questionnaire, his points were presented. They generated some interest and discussion, but also a fair amount of disagreement His methods are:

1. Become genuinely interested in other people.
2. Smile.
3. Remember that a person's name is to that person the sweetest and most important sound in any language.
4. Be a good listener. ...
5. Talk in terms of the other person's interests.
6. Make the other person feel important - and do it sincerely.

Carnegie was eventually dropped from the discussions as it was thought that he showed a somewhat cynical attitude in using one's friends. It was replaced by Marcus Tullius Cicero, who wrote a book on friendship (*De Amicitia*) from which you can find over a dozen or more rules on what constitutes a good friendship. One rule that this writer has adopted, and has come to believe in, over the years is, if there is a genuine interest in the other, and in what he or she is doing, then make the effort to keep the friendship alive by continuing the contact, year in and year out.

Chapter 8

RELIGION,
A HEALTHY LIFE, AND DEATH

One of the major reasons for unhappiness in old age is the infirmities of ageing, and the consequences that come with it. First, however, I need to look at one of the issues that came up in the research on those issues – religion.

Older adults who participate in private religious activity appear to have a survival advantage over those who do not. Several studies suggesting that church going, religious beliefs, and prayer can improve morbidity and mortality. These studies have increasingly received attention in medical journals and the general media. For the most part, they support the contention that religious practices can extend life. A six-year follow-up study of 3,851 older adults in North Carolina was initiated in 1986 and followed for 6 years. Level of participation in private religious activities such as prayer, meditation, or bible study was assessed by self-reporting. This information formed the baseline, along with a wide variety of sociodemographic and health variables.

The main outcome measure was time (days) to death[1]. In the median 6.3-year follow-up period, 1,137 subjects (29.5%) died. Those reporting rarely to never participating in private religious activity had an increased relative hazard of dying over more frequently attending participants, although this hazard did not remain significant for the sample after adjustment for demographic and health variables. When the sample was divided into activity of daily living (ADL) impaired and unimpaired, the effect did not remain significant for the ADL impaired group. The conclusion reached by the study authors, however, was that older adults who participate in private religious activity before the onset of ADL impairment appear to have a survival advantage over those who do not.

A study published in the US journal *Demography* also found that:

> *People who never attend (religious service) exhibit 1.87 times the risk of death in the follow-up period compared with people who attend more than once a week. This translates into a seven-year difference in life expectancy at age 20 between those who never attend and those who attend more than once a week.*[2]

In another 20-year study, Harvard scientists found that women who went to religious services twice a week were one-third less likely to die compared to non-attendees[3] That study also referred to another study at Duke University that concluded that steady church attendance improves health and prolongs life.[4] Other convincing literature indicates that involvement in religion is associated with good health throughout adult life. See Koenig, McCullough, & Larson (2001) for a review of this research[5].

It should not be accepted that this author is advocating that we take up religion as a way to a longer and healthier life. There are five sets of information to consider before making that decision. One is that countries with very low life expectancy are mostly religious. The nations of sub-Saharan Africa are a good example. Malaria, dengue fever, cholera, diarrheal diseases, HIV/AIDS, etc., lop decades off life expectancy. It is below 60 years for most of these countries. Many African people practise traditional African religions, along with a variety of Christian religions.[6] South American countries, mostly Catholic, are also examples. The exception is the United States - the most church going country in the western world [7]. Sixty percent of Americans say that religion is "very important" to them; only 21 percent of Western Europeans say that. To be noted is that Americans live about 2 years less than their counterparts in high-income countries in Europe and Asia. American men and women can only look forward to a life expectancy of 76.4 and 81.2 years, respectively, compared with the 78.6 and 83.4 years of their peers abroad. Drugs, guns, poor diet, and motor vehicles are largely to blame, some studies find [8]. It should be noticed, however, that the above life expectancy and religion studies are all US based where religion has a high visibility and commitment. Possibly the lifestyles of many Americans may be throwing away the advantages the country gains from its religious commitment.

One other consideration is that religion, for many, is a driving force in their lives. It may take the place of the all-consuming activity advocated by the positive psychologists. A third consideration, and perhaps of some significance, is that churches promote a virtuous life, "to do unto others as you would have others do to you". This concept encourages the virtuous life endorsed by Aristotle and repeated by today's positive psychologists.

Finally, Pascal's wager must be mentioned. Blaise Pascal (1623-1662) offered a pragmatic reason for believing in God. Even under the assumption that God's existence is unlikely, he argued that it is wiser to believe in God and practise religion. Nothing is lost if God does not exist, and you go to heaven, not hell, if he does exist.[9] This writer will accept that God may allow you to enter heaven if He knew you were a non-believer who professed a belief in Him. Whether God would give you an extra two years of life if you are a non-believer, professing a belief, is open to doubt. Pascal did not explore this option.

The fifth reason is you may be able to pick the eye teeth out of the various religions. Today, many young people are leaving the faith-based religions.[10] The reasons appear to be several: difficulty in believing in a God, a disconnect with the teachings of the various churches, a heartlessness on some social issues, particularly gay marriage, by some religions. Yet religious institutions supply many of our charitable activities. It may be a worthwhile occupation for the after 65 years to find that combination of religious beliefs that meet your needs and beliefs. See Ronald Dworkin's "Religion without God" and the many discussions it has generated.

A HEALTHY LIFE

It was Cicero who first told us, over 2000 years ago, that for a long and healthy life, we should eat well and take exercise. But he did not tell us what to eat and how much exercise. That is the purpose of this section. It is advice that you will find in the newspapers almost daily. This section, however, has an ulterior motive - to find interesting and attractive foods, and to determine what is the minimum amount of exercise that you can get away with. On the enjoyable foods list is popcorn (home-made, not movie popcorn), chocolate and red wine, grass fed beef, canned salmon, purple potatoes, oysters, strawberries, blackberries and mangos. The benefits of these foods can be checked out on any website. There are many more, including several different types of interesting and tasty green vegetables.

The benefits of red wine are clear, but it does have to be in moderation - one drink per day for women and two drinks per day for men, or less. And the chocolate should be dark chocolate.

Exercise is trickier. A Canadian study recommendation for older adults includes moderately vigorous cardiorespiratory activities (e.g., brisk walking), strength and (or) power training for maintenance of muscle mass and specific muscle-group performance, as well as "balance-mobility practice" and flexibility (stretching) exercise.[11] That study recommends "30–60 minutes of *moderate* activity most days of the week"; walking, with "progress to moderate or brisk pace." Strengthening exercises using "a weight that will *challenge your muscles*" (weights that can be lifted 10 times before they become too heavy) are recommended. Flexibility or stretching and balance activities are included. That publication (which can be found on the net along with many others) describes several recommendations from different sources around the world, in reaching the above conclusions.

The New York Times on June 20, 2016 carried an article: "The case for exercising: If the effects of exercise "could be put in a pill and prescribed, it would be rightly hailed as an almost miraculous cure". Exercise lowered the pain and improved the function of patients with osteoarthritis of the knee. It also increases aerobic capacity and muscle strength in patients with rheumatoid arthritis. For people (mostly middle-aged men) who had had a heart attack, exercise therapy reduced all causes of mortality by 27 percent and cardiac mortality by 31 percent. Fourteen additional controlled trials showed physiological benefits in those with heart failure. Exercise has also been shown to lower blood pressure in patients with hypertension, and improve cholesterol and triglyceride levels.

People with diabetes who exercise have lower HbA1c values, which is the marker of blood sugar control, low enough to probably reduce the risk of complications from the disease.

How much do you have to do? The New York Times tells us that 150 minutes per week of moderate intensity physical activity for adults, or about 30 minutes each weekday is enough. Moderate intensity is probably much less than you think. Walking briskly, at 3 to 4 miles per hour or so, qualifies. So does bicycling slower than 10 miles an hour. Anything that gets your heart rate somewhere between 110 and 140 beats per minute is enough.

Older people do have increasing health problems. They need to keep abreast of their aches and pains. There are many answers on the web. The website that the author's family uses is Web MD, a US based health advisory company. It does have several pages of advice for older people and it can even send you a daily newsletter with health tips. This writer does not subscribe but is aware of several people who do. Web MD is only one of several health advisory websites. For no other reason than older people have more health problems, they, along with a willingness to readily consult their local general practitioner, will assist in building a longer and healthier, and with that, a happier old age.

MINDFULNESS AND MEDITATION

This section on health, even though it is for older people, would not be complete without a discussion on these interrelated topics. They appear to be the latest craze. In 2014, the UK parliament set up the Mindfulness All-Party Parliamentary Group to consider mindfulness. Initiated by Lord Richard Layard, one of the positive psychologists mentioned earlier, and a Labour MP, it undertook a year of research and eight hearings and then released an extensive report in October 2015. It described mindfulness as an "important innovation in mental health".[12] They found that mindfulness "has the potential to help many people to better health and flourishing." They defined mindfulness as "paying attention to what's happening in the present moment in the mind, body and external environment, with an attitude of curiosity and kindness." They do say, however, that "We are aware that the current popularity of mindfulness is running ahead of the research evidence."

This is an issue replicated in some newspaper articles. One asks "Is mindfulness all it's cracked up to be? Adherents of mindfulness credit it with everything from lifting depression to improving military capability. But is it just psychology's latest trend?"[13] It reaches the conclusion that mindfulness has become, according to US religious scholar David McMahan, "one of these things that can have many meanings and many uses for different people". This has led to Dr Miles Neale, a Buddhist psychotherapist, dubbing it "McMindfulness". He links meditation and mindfulness together.[14]

The Harvard Medical School also has published the results of a conference on mindfulness which has the finding "How mindfulness can change your brain and improve your health."[15]

This author decided to find out for himself. After spending several hundred dollars on three courses, including one combined meditation cum mindfulness course, concluded that it is a great bore. The first short course sent him to sleep. The several sessions in the longer course spent contemplating different parts of your body, or listening to your own breathing, seemed to him a complete waste of time. The alternate meditating contemplations on the meaning of friendship appeared to have greater potential, but along with the instruction to empty your mind of all stray thoughts, did not achieve a great deal in practice.

But his is not a universal conclusion. One of the research interviewees who had spent 10 days meditating in silence, without talking to the other attendees, or any communication with the outside world, was convinced of the benefits. She reached a degree of inner peace with herself, including finally saying goodbye to two people who had been important in her life.

This author, however, is not convinced. Meditation apps are available for your smartphone. Using one in yet another trial attempt, the net effect was again to fall asleep. Readers are advised that they will need to try mindfulness for themselves.

As an encouragement to do so, readers are reminded of the links between Stoicism and mindfulness. Stoicism was founded by Zeno in Cyprus (344–262 BCE), and elaborated by Cleanthes (d. 232 BCE) and Chrysippus (d. ca. 206 BCE). According to the Stanford Encyclopedia of Philosophy, Stoicism the name derives from the porch in the Agora at Athens decorated with mural paintings, where the members of the school congregated, and their lectures were held. The English adjective 'stoical' is indicative of its beliefs. The Stoics did, in fact, hold that emotions like fear or envy (or impassioned sexual attachments, or passionate love of anything whatsoever) either were, or arose from, false judgements and that the sage—a person who had attained moral and intellectual perfection—would not undergo them.

Mindfulness is similar. One belief in the practice is that it relieves us from tension and the anxiety of our daily life. The fact that this experimenter fell asleep is certainly an indication that it does relieve tension.

The links with Buddhism are more obvious. Meditation is of Buddhist origins. We are all aware of the Buddha meditating, searching for enlightenment. The course that this writer went on was labelled a Mindfulness/Meditation course.

Christianity also has embraced meditation. It was explored by saints such as Ignatius of Loyola and Teresa of Avila in the 16th century.[16] They saw it as the practice of reading, thinking, praying and contemplating. These views make much greater sense to this writer, for you are not listing to your breathing, or contemplating your feet. You are meditating on issues of concern to you.

To repeat, the reader is advised to try for themselves.

PET DOGS & HEALTH

I long debated with members of my family on whether a paragraph or two on dogs would fit in this health section. My reasons were the emotional kicks and companionship, even love, that a pet dog would give you, along with the exercise. They do have to be walked each day. I even wondered whether I should write that they would be great companions for people now living on their own.

Before making the decision, I decided to look up the research on this subject. The answer was clear. Your pet is a necessary part of a healthy life. A publication of the Harvard Medical School tells us that:

- Dog owners are less likely to suffer from depression than those without pets.
- People with dogs have lower blood pressure in stressful situations than those without pets. One study even found that when people with borderline hypertension adopted dogs from a shelter, their blood pressure declined significantly within five months.
- Playing with a dog or cat can elevate levels of serotonin and dopamine, which calm and relax.
- Pet owners have lower triglyceride and cholesterol levels (indicators of heart disease) than those without pets.
- Heart attack patients with dogs survive longer than those without.
- Pet owners over age 65 make 30 percent fewer visits to their doctors than those without pets.[17]

In fact, the medical school provides three pages of information on your life with a dog. It also, it should be added, has a very positive section on mindfulness, noted above. It uses the term mindfulness meditation to describe the practice.

It is not the only study with these results. A three-year study of 5741 people by the Baker Medical Research Institute in Melbourne showed that pet owners had lower blood pressure, triglyceride and cholesterol levels than non-owners.[18]

Ownership benefits the dog, but it depends on how you talk to them. Scientists at the University of York have shown that using 'dog-speak' to communicate with dogs (such as 'that's a good boy' in somewhat of a baby talk tone) is important in relationship-building between pet and owner, similar to the way that type of talking establishes a bond between a baby and an adult.[19]

Psychology Today also confirms the benefits of pet ownership. Their initial documenting of the positive findings is under the heading of pets, but many of the actual benefits are attributed to dog ownership.[20] I am not going to enter a dispute about a dog as a pet versus a cat, for the findings are clear. If you are on your own, and do not like it, seek out a puppy to keep you company. The love you give will be returned twenty times over.

If your apartment or housing estate will not permit a dog, sell your house. Try to find a new place that will permit you to keep your dog.

DIFFICULTIES IN LIFE

One of the many contributors to the discussions on these topics, Hazel, 71, has argued that under adverse circumstances you can never be happy. Her example was if your children are taken away from you, by war, or by a plague that was sweeping the country, you are then certainly not happy. And it does not matter how virtuous you are, how much you try to help others, you are in fact devastated.

It is an issue that Cicero tackled two thousand years ago. In an article W*hether virtue alone be sufficient for a happy life*[21].Cicero, in his reply to his colleague Brutus, who says that virtue is of itself insufficient for a happy life, responded that virtue is sufficient. Cicero does admit some doubt, due to the many and various strokes of fortune, that when he reflects "on those troubles with which I have been so severely exercised by fortune, I begin to distrust this opinion" (that virtue is sufficient for a happy life). He adds that "nature had given us infirm bodies and had joined to them incurable diseases and intolerable pains" as further reason for distrusting the opinion on the value of virtue. Cicero, however, starts to bring in the benefits of Stoicism. Brutus then adds in torture: *"a man may display all these qualities (constancy, and dignity, and wisdom, and courage) on the rack; but yet the rack is inconsistent with a happy life."*

"...these arguments of the Stoics are pleasanter to taste than to swallow."

Cicero is an extremely verbose writer, referencing in his support, people and incidents in Roman history of whom the ordinary reader has never heard. Identifying his precise opinions and his responses takes some searching. He concludes this argument, however, by asserting his stoic beliefs.

> *Those are happy, who are alarmed by no fears, wasted by no griefs, provoked by no lusts, melted by no languid pleasures that arise from vain and exulting joys.*

And again:

> *Why do...the Stoics say so much on that question, whether virtue was abundantly sufficient to a happy life?*
> *If we were to allow poverty, obscurity, humility, solitude, the loss of friends, acute pains of the body, the loss of health, weakness, blindness, the ruin of one's country, banishment, slavery, to be evils: for a wise man may be afflicted by all these evils, numerous and im-*

> *portant as they are, and many others also may be added; for they are brought on by chance, which may attack a wise man.*

Cicero goes on at length to discuss this issue, concluding "that neither the attacks of fortune, nor the opinion of the multitude, nor pain, nor poverty, occasion them (a wise man) any apprehensions".

Stoicism, in essence, has the same meaning in Cicero's time as today. He strongly advocated wisdom and forbearance. That happiness for humans is found in accepting that which we have been given in life, by not allowing ourselves to be controlled by our preferences or desires. This advice of Cicero warrants some consideration by older people, for they are the ones afflicted by the increasing infirmity of the added years. What Cicero is saying is essentially "Grin and bear it."

It is advice that this writer has heard in several of the discussions with older people and is one which he supports totally.

Cicero ends his examination of virtue by introducing us to the problems of our own deaths, the topic of the next section

> *I am persuaded that we are prepared and fortified sufficiently for our own death, or that of our friends, against grief and the other perturbations of the mind.*

DEATH

This will be a short section for the reason that nobody in the survey listed it as a concern. This writer also does not think that death is a serious issue. Cicero, as we know, also stated that it is not a problem that we should worry about. And we do not even have to adopt stoic thinking to relegate our views on our death to the back recesses of our minds. Aristotle and Plato even believed that we have a soul, which for some observers, is a form of afterlife, and thereby implying that death does not exist. Aristotle even wrote a book on the soul (*De Anima*). He believed, however, that the soul died with you. As noted earlier, most religions and most believers, are convinced that the soul is everlasting.

This chapter, therefore, will end by describing a number of deaths, all philosophers. One is that of Epicurus, (341—271 B.C.) who had his own school of philosophy, and who is credited by John Stuart Mill as the founder of utilitarianism. He wrote that we need not fear death. On his deathbed, he penned this short letter to Idomeneus, a member of his philosophy school:

> *On this blissful day, which is also the last of my life, I write this to you. My continual sufferings from strangury and dysentery are so great that nothing could increase them; but I set above them all the gladness of mind at the memory of our past conversations. But I would have you, as becomes your lifelong attitude to me and to philosophy; watch over the children of Metrodorus*[22]

Another is the death of David Hume. The following is an extract from a letter written by his doctor to Adam Smith:

> Edinburgh, Monday, 26th August, 1776.
> "DEAR SIR, — Yesterday, about four o'clock, afternoon, Mr. Hume expired. The near approach of his death became evident in the night between Thursday and Friday, when his disease became excessive, and soon weakened him so much that he could no longer rise out of his bed. He continued to the last perfectly sensible, and free from much pain or feelings of distress. He never dropped the smallest expression of impatience; but when he had occasion to speak to the people about him, always did it with affection and tenderness. I thought it improper to write to bring you over, especially as I heard that he had dictated a letter to you desiring you not to come. When he became very weak, it cost him an effort to speak, and he died in such a happy composure of mind, that nothing could exceed it."

It was Hume who argued that our ethical behaviour is based on emotion or sentiment rather than on abstract moral principles. He proclaimed that "Reason is, and ought only to be the slave of the passions." This is an issue examined in some depth in the Afterword to this book.

The above two were philosophers. Writers on philosophy seem to delight about writing on the deaths of their fellow philosophers. Others worth mentioning are:

- (399 BC) Socrates, condemned to death by 500 of his fellow Athenians, despite a vigorous defence claiming his innocence, refused the chance to escape, as he believed his civic duty was to obey the wishes of his fellow citizens. His taking of hemlock is described by Plato in *The Crito*.

- (1535) Thomas More, Lord High Chancellor of England from 1529 to 1532 was executed by beheading in 1535 for refusing to acknowledge King Henry VIII. as Supreme Head of the Church of England and the annulment of his marriage to Catherine of Aragon. He is the author of *Utopia*, More's theory on what constitutes the perfect world. This writer, if faced with beheading as an alternative to acknowledging the king's requests, would quickly concede. This story is included only to add strength to this section's essence that death is not of great importance to many philosophers.

- (1650) René Descartes normally stayed in bed to noon, thinking great thoughts. Credited with being the "Father of Modern Philosophy," he is the originator of the phrase "I think, Therefore I am," from which he developed an argument that proved the existence of god[23]. Many observers, including this one, believe that the argument is circular. He argues for the existence of a benevolent God, to defeat his sceptical argument in his first Meditation that God might be a deceiver[24]. Descartes also believed in the immortality of the soul, which he located halfway between your ears. He was later asked to instruct Queen Christina of Sweden in philosophy starting at 5 am, he caught pneumonia on the way to work in the middle of a Swedish winter (this was the father of Western philosophy!). He died in February 1650.

Chapter 9

THE ROLE OF GOVERNMENT

In *De Legibus*, Cicero wrote, "Let the welfare of the people be the ultimate law". Cicero wrote this work as a dialogue between himself, his brother Quintus and their friend Atticus. They were important people in Cicero's life. The dialogue begins with the three of them in Cicero's family estate at Arpinum, outside Rome. As mentioned in an earlier chapter, Cicero made his statement on the obligations of government on several occasions.

Plato also made this claim, several centuries before Cicero. *Our object in the construction of the state is the greatest happiness of the whole, and not that of any one class.* (The Republic, Book IV). We saw Aristotle's disagreement with the proposals of Plato in Chapter 2. But that was a disagreement with the methods proposed by Plato, not with the obligation on government to ensure our happiness. The Stanford Encyclopedia of Philosophy tells us that Aristotle also was concerned about happiness and the role of government[1]: "The theme that the good life or happiness is the proper end of the city-state recurs throughout Aristotle's *Politics*".

Thomas Jefferson also said, "The care of life and happiness is the sole legitimate objective of government" It was Jefferson who placed the "pursuit of happiness" as a basic right in the US Declaration of Independence.

John Locke thought that the purpose of government was to protect the *natural rights* of its citizens. He said that natural rights were life, liberty and property, and that all people automatically earned these simply by being born. Depending on how we fully interpret natural rights, however, will decide how we interpret Locke's views. The 1948 United Nations Universal Declaration of Human Rights is an instrument enshrining the concept of natural rights. The 30 articles of the Declaration, if observed, would certainly guarantee that no act of other human beings would jeopardise the possibility of a happy life.

Thomas More wrote his book *Utopia* on the ideal modern state. It has since been criticised as a satire. The observations of this reviewer are that More's Utopian thoughts were created in a flight of unimaginable fantasy.

Or, if More was serious, then his thoughts are somewhat ambiguous. A major theme of More's earlier work, however, *The History of King Richard III*, was on the deception and ruthlessness of rulers, so his thoughts then were in the right place. In *Utopia*, his ideas are open to question. But they do leave with us the concept that many, if not all of us, desire a world that is better than what we have. In short, More is also saying that our happiness is one responsibility of our governments. He references this thought primarily through his promulgation of the law in Utopia for the good of the people. He notes that representatives from neighbouring countries visited Utopia and invited the Utopian magistrates to come and help establish similar systems of law in their own countries.

Several modern psychologists also make the assertion that assuring our happiness is a task of government. Richard Layard, on a London School of Economics website, for instance, clearly makes the statement:

> *Government's role should be to increase happiness and reduce misery. Policy outcomes must change to reflect outcomes in terms of changes to happiness.*

Unfortunately, his article only explores some of the issues behind this contention. It does not fully explain how it might be achieved.

This chapter attempts that exploration. It faces many issues. First is defining happiness in a way that connects sensibly with the possible actions of a government. Layard has said "Happiness is a feeling, and there is a spectrum running from extreme happiness at one end to extreme misery at the other. Happiness is feeling good and enjoying your life and wanting to go on that way".

But that definition does not help that much in determining what policies a government might adopt in encouraging or promoting happiness. This book to date has reached the conclusion that we are happiest, most fulfilled, if we are engaged in activities that are important to us, that demand, and receive, our commitment and time. That definition, however, also does not provide us with any guidance on how a government might ensure happiness in its people.

This chapter, therefore, is only the beginnings of that exploration. It starts, however, with the concept that an overriding obligation of government is to ensure that we come to no harm. And if we do suffer from some harm, whether by accident of birth, by the onslaught of a disease, by natural or civil disturbance, then it is the obligation of government to mitigate that harm.

The concept that "Our prime purpose in life is to help others, and if you cannot help them, at least don't harm them" is I believe, a universal ethical obligation on us, as well as on our governments. This obligation has been examined in greater detail in the Afterword. Those who have read the works of even a few moral philosophers will realise that this obligation is a massive simplification of the multitude of moral theories that have been developed by philosophers over the centuries. The reasoning behind this obligation is a separate exercise in moral philosophy, and consequently has been placed in the Afterword to this book.

It cannot be denied, however, that our happiness in old age, or in any age for that matter, will be increased if Governments work towards ensuring that no harm comes to us, or if we have already suffered some harm then it is a government's role to help alleviate that harm. It is also our own obligation. The Afterword expands this obligation to include all of us. To help others, not to harm them is in fact, a universal obligation drawn from the moral philosophies across the globe, both Western and Eastern. The Afterword further explores the moral reasoning that will help resolve many of our current issues – same-sex marriage, euthanasia, universal health care, capital punishment, abortion, designer babies and others. It has been placed as a separate part of the book for two reasons: One is that it defines a virtuous life- a requirement that many philosophers and modern-day psychologists have told us is necessary for a happy life. Secondly and equally importantly, is that it gives us the reasoning behind adopting the rule that our moral obligation is to help others, or at least not to harm them. This guideline provides us at least one rule by which governments may ensure our happiness.

What then is the role of government(s)?

"to increase happiness and reduce misery " is Richard Layard's answer to this question, repeated in similar terms by a number of psychologists and philosophers over the centuries. To begin to find an answer to the question "What is the role of government," I will start by identifying the major issues facing the world. Resolving those issues will bring about a greater happiness for many people. The findings of an Australian think tank - The Australia Institute, is a beginning. It finds that eight major problems are facing that country (Figure 9.1). Most of these issues have moral implications, in that they affect the well-being and happiness of the people in Australian communities. A couple are economic priorities.

**Figure 9.1
Australian priorities
The Australia Institute**

1. Global warming
2. Budgeting and the economy
3. Inequality
4. Retirement & superannuation
5. Refugees/asylum seekers
6. The land; protecting the environment
7. Protecting the ABC / SBS (Public Broadcasters)
8. Free Trade

The United Nations has conducted a global survey of people's priorities for a better world. It reflects a higher value placed on jobs and food than does the Australia Institute. It is available on the web under "United Nations, My World" The ranking of the priorities is summarised in Figure 9.2 below.

**Figure 9.2
Unted Nations.
Global Survey of the World's Priorities**

1. A good education
2. Better health care
3. Better job opportunities
4. An honest and responsive government
5. Affordable and nutritious food
6. Protection against crime and violence
7. Access to clean water and sanitation
8. Support for people who cannot work
9. Equality between men and women
10. Better transport and roads
11. Reliable energy at home
12. Freedom from discrimination and persecution
13. Political freedoms
14. Protecting forests, rivers and oceans
15. Phone and internet access
16. Action on climate change

Priorities for Britain and the United States are somewhat similar to Australia. Britain has a Government Communications Plan, as well as one published by McKinsey & Co., a management consulting group. The United States has many action groups attempting to influence government priorities. They would primarily be advocating economic or social priorities.

The ranking of the priorities of items by the western nations and the United Nations are informative. Once we inject into our analysis the needs of people in the developing countries, we find that the overall priorities change. Those of us living in a developed country, with some degree of education and affluence, have different priorities to those in countries where food and clean water are priority needs for well-being.

The World Economic Forum's ranking of the challenges facing the world illustrates these differences:

1. Ending hunger, achieving food security and improving nutrition.
2. Creating jobs. More than 200 million people are unemployed globally.
3. Climate change.
4. Global Financial Management. Several years after the Global Financial crisis, the world economy is still struggling with slow growth, unconventional monetary policy and constrained government budgets
5. The internet. Digital technologies cannot help but disrupt our existing models of business and government.
6. Gender equality. It isn't just a moral issue, the Forum asserts, it makes economic sense.
7. Investing for the long term- a change that is vital for economic growth and social well-being.
8. Serious challenges to global health remain. The number of people on the planet is set to rise to 9.7 billion in 2050 with 2 billion aged over 60.

The priorities of the readers of this book are again likely to be different. Most likely live in a reasonably developed community, where food, water and sanitation are given – such facilities are readily available and will not be necessary for your well-being. Remember that a dominant finding coming out of this book is that peoples' happiness or fulfilment came from a commitment to an activity that demanded their full attention. Although these commitments were different for different people, they were still a far cry from the needs of the poor in developing countries. These demands are more basic – food and shelter.

Overriding all demands, however, must be a commitment not to harm people, and in addition to that commitment, a further commitment to help those who need help. Those demands also apply to governments. Deciding what is the prioritisation of these demands is a basic problem of democratic government. Possibly at the top is the commitment to prevent war. But there are additional issues. We have seen major differences of opinion in recent years, with the rise of populist and far right governments, all having very differing opinions on what is best for the country. Along with them have come attempts to change priorities. Examples are (i) the reduction of a universal health care system in the United States, (ii) Brexit – the leaving the European Union in the United Kingdom, with its attendant reduction in national well-being, and (iii) modification of the racial discrimination Act in Australia. The treatment of refugees, global warming, and managing terrorism are also issues for all countries. How governments best contribute to our universal happiness is not an easy task to resolve.

The author's reflections in the next chapter attempt to bring together the findings of the three sources of information used in this book – the philosophers over history, the modern day positive psychologists and the surveys of those already over 65. These reflections further identify different demands on us and on our governments. But before we make that survey, we need to discuss one looming difference in the English-speaking world – the Intergenerational gap. The different outlook on the world, the conflicting demands on the world between the young and the old.

The Generation Gap

A generation gap or generational gap, is a difference of opinion between one generation and another regarding beliefs, politics, or values. One reason behind the gap appears that old people tend to be conservative, often supporting policies and practices of past years. The two generations have different, and at times have different values, giving rise to conflicting demands on the world.

I will deal with the conservative issue first. This tendency is often evidenced in voting patterns, but they also arise in public demonstrations and even in direct confrontation. There were two causes behind Britain's Brexit vote. One was a desire to limit foreign immigration through Europe but the second was the desire of the older generation to return to a Britain that they knew in their youth.[2] This second reason has created problems for the next generation, an issue discussed in the second part of this section on inter-generational conflict.

The same tendency is seen in Australia. A Crosby Textor poll in July 2014 showed that the lowest support for same sex marriage came from Australians aged over 65, at 48 per cent, and men over 55, at 42 per cent.[3] Although the results of the national plebiscite now out, we are unfortunately, unable to distinguish the age voting patterns for the historic yes" vote in favour of same sex marriage (by a substantial margin of 61.6 per cent to 38.4 percent).

The British Guardian Newspaper tells us that "Conventional wisdom: People turn Tory with age."[4] It applies worldwide. A Washington State University article "Age Gap? The Influence of Age on Voting Behavior and Political Preferences in the American Electorate" tells us that "In 2008 and 2012, younger people overwhelmingly voted for Democrat Barack Obama, while older people instead voted for Republicans John McCain and Mitt Romney by wide margins."

The November 2016 election was similarly influenced by older voters. A University of Virginia Center for Politics poll of Trump voters shows.[5]

> *— The breakdown of strong approvers vs. somewhat approvers largely mirrored Trump's relative areas of strength and weakness in the campaign amongst the broader electorate: Men were likelier to be strong approvers than women (44% of men were strong approvers vs. 39% of women); respondents over 65 were the only age group where strong approvers outnumbered somewhat approvers (48%-46%); and, amongst respondents with differing levels of education, strong approvers narrowly outnumbered somewhat approvers only amongst those with a high school education or less (49%-47%), while voters with at least some college education were likelier to somewhat approve than strongly approve*

That same Guardian article tells us that the voting patterns of individuals in eight post-Soviet countries in the elections of 1989 or 1990 reveal disproportionately conservative (in the sense of preserving the status quo) voting among older voters. The French newspaper *Le Figaro* gave us the same message about the recent French elections: "Those more than 65 years of age are the group most supportive for the candidate of the right and centre.[6] This candidate was Francois Fillon, who, as some may know, lost the election due to accusations that he used public money to pay his family for work that they had never done.

If these observations are correct, and they appear to be, it would seem that the demands of older people on their governments will not tend to encourage a movement for change. Remember that Aristotle said, 2500 years ago, that old people are 'Driven too much by the useful; not enough by the noble'. That is unfortunate for there is much about our current world where change for the better has a high priority.

The generation gap is a far more serious issue. Brexit is possibly the strongest example in the Western world. The report of the All Party Parliamentary Group on Social Integration[7] points out that the split between the young and old generations was expressed forcefully in the verdict offered by each generation at last year's referendum on the United Kingdom's membership of the European Union. There can be no denying that Brexit is something of an intergenerational sore spot. Many younger Remain supporters feel that their futures have been sold down the river by their Leave-voting elders. They are not wrong to believe that large numbers of Baby Boomers and members of the Greatest Generation (those born from the early 1900s up to the mid-1920s) are inclined to prioritise Brexiting above all else.[8]

New research conducted by YouGov and The Challenge on behalf of the APPG on Social Integration shows that 28% of Leave voters of retirement age believe that lower wages for the next generation would for be a price worth paying for Britain's departure from the European Union.[9] In fact, more Leave voters aged 65 and over agree with this proposition than disagree. Equally strikingly, a similar number (28%) of Remain-backers aged 18 to 34 would be willing to see pensions for older people reduced if it meant a stop to Brexit.[10]

The chair of the Parliamentary group Chuka Umunna MP, in his introduction, told of a visit to Boston in Lincolnshire, the local authority area which voted to leave the EU by the greatest margin.

> *Instead, the majority of the older Bostonians who I spoke with told me that they had voted for Brexit for a variety of reasons unrelated to race. Some voiced concerns about public services pushed to the brink by a growing population, whilst others spoke about national sovereignty. Many said they had backed the Leave campaign exactly because they were worried about the impact of economic migration on the earning power and futures of their children and grandchildren. Some felt that their town had changed beyond recognition in a short space of time and had 'stopped feeling like home' – they remembered fondly a time during which they had known their neighbours and felt that their community had been hollowed out.*

THE ROLE OF GOVERNMENT 81

The same generation gap seen in other countries. It is the young still of school age that are taking on the lobbying power of the National Rifle Association. The massacre at Marjory Stoneman Douglas High School in Parkland, Florida, which left 17 dead, may well become the catalyst that will undermine the power of the gun lobby in America. "We are going to be the last mass shooting," High School student Emma Gonzalez shouted at a packed rally in Fort Lauderdale recently. "We are going to change the laws." Survivors and other students have created #NeverAgain, a movement that has gained attention in social and traditional media, sparking TV interviews, viral videos, a march, and support from celebrities. Some of the banners have advertised the fact that it is the students that are being killed – that expressions of condolence are useless in stopping the massacres.

A different generational gap issue is seen in Australia, where the current party in opposition has committed to a change in tax policy should it win government. The new policy is to remove the reimbursement of taxes paid by corporations when shares in those corporations form part of the private investments used by people to finance their retirement. Australia introduced the scheme, termed dividend imputation, to offset the tax paid by Australian residents who owned shares on which tax had already been paid by the company. The scheme was introduced by earlier governments when the economy was booming. Designed to encourage people to self-fund their retirements, the scheme paid back to the self-funded retirement scheme any corporate taxes paid in their investments. But once the self-funded scheme goes into the payout phase, it pays no taxes. But the tax office still paid back the previously paid corporate taxes. Although the change is fair and just, massive objection to the tax change has been launched by retirees, and by the current government. The Conversation calls the changes intergenerational theft.[11] One blog calls it *The great retiree blame game.*[12] The Institute of Public Affairs (IPA), a right wing think tank has declared war on the proposed changes to super. The effect, however, of the continuation of dividend imputation for non-tax paying retirees, will result in a disproportionate share of government funding being born by the younger generation to benefit older people. No other country which has a dividend imputation scheme extends the payment to a person who does not pay tax.

This chapter has added only fractionally to the overall discussion. Many will say, in any case, that older people have little influence on what governments can do to make them happy. The chapter has been written to point out an alternative. Older people do vote, and they do influence government. And that this influence is not always in the interests of the wider society. Those seeking an activity to which they would like to commit time and energy could consider ways in which they, and their government could work towards the society that Plato, Aristotle, Cicero, along with many Asian philosophers, called for many years ago.

Chapter 10

BRINGING IT TOGETHER

The previous chapters have documented the findings of many different observers, from the Greek philosophers two thousand years before now, to the very latest from the modern psychological researchers. The third source was the views of over 150 people over 65 on why this period is the happiest time of their lives. This chapter attempts to draw out the overriding conclusions.

A note of caution is in order. Remember that the initial drive to research this book was the rejection of the widely accepted belief that older people are less than fully happy. In other words, this writer started off with the bias that the majority of older people could, and do, lead happy and fulfilling lives. Nevertheless, a writer cannot spend the weeks and months digging into theses research findings from so many sources without being pushed towards reaching some worthwhile findings.

This chapter attempts to develop the core findings. And present them in some sort of priority order. Every attempt will be made to avoid any subjective assessment of personal happiness and well-being.

What did the investigations conclude? Summarising the positive psychologists, together with the early Greek writers and fitting them in with the questionnaire findings is not a straightforward task. There is much in agreement but also considerable disagreement.

At the top of this listing of activities that bring happiness to the over 65s must go an activity, or activities, that are important to you. This conclusion is in fact, a conclusion that is valid throughout your whole life. That activity can be one, or several, but they must occupy a large segment of your time and attention. This is a concept that was endorsed by the positive psychologists. The term I have used to describe this activity is your Project - your big project, or projects, in life. Or at least for the current period in your life. The many discussions that accompanied this investigation suggest that there can be several at any one time, and that they can change. If you get fed up with one, then drop it. That recommendation would also apply for the years earlier than 65, when your work can occupy much of your attention. If it is not as fulfilling as you would like it to be, seek another job. Even seek another career.

What makes for a happy, flourishing life in a later age in life is finding that activity (or activities), after retirement, that becomes a project to which you are fully committed. It is your 'project'…or projects…. something bigger than yourself, pursued for its own sake. This conclusion is the overriding finding of this book.

The surveys supplied by the over 65 respondents along with that of the positive psychologists initially appear to near totally contrast this view. At the top of the survey respondents' list is freedom, freedom to do anything or everything that they want to do. This dominant response from the personal questionnaires – that the post sixty-five years are the best years because you are free to do anything you want – does appear to contradict the ancient Greek philosophers as well as the positive psychologists. Neither of the latter two groups specified freedom. But these apparently opposing sets of answers are not inconsistent. Free time permits you to pursue activities that are important to you – a position that reflects the recommendations of the ancient philosophers as well as the positive psychologists. And because you now have the time, the post 65 years are more enjoyable than before. The issue is identifying those activities that are fulfilling; that are important to you.

Travel is high up the responses to the questionnaire - again a unique response. In the interviews that accompanied the survey, this writer discussed travel with several respondents who rated it highly. For some of the sixty-five plus respondents it was near a full-time activity, - planning their trips (including a search for the minimum cost option), before embarking on their cruise, or setting off in their grey nomad camper van, would occupy the larger part of their year. The reasons behind their enjoyment included the new experiences that travel brings.

If we turn now to the positive psychologists and the philosophers, both old and new, we get a different picture

Learning or curiosity is high on the modern psychologists' findings, and on the respondents' answers. This conclusion, that curiosity has a high input to our happiness, puts a heavy weight on Seligman's PERMA - Positive Emotion, Engagement, Relationships, Meaning, Accomplishments. Seligman's PERMA does not mention curiosity. If we dig into PERMA, perhaps the closest we can find is engagement. The Positive Psychology website describes engagement as:

> *We all need something in our lives that entirely absorbs us into the present moment, creating a 'flow' of blissful immersion into the task or activity. This type of 'flow' of engagement is important to stretch our intelligence, skills, and emotional capabilities.*

Which is not quite the same as curiosity. The explanation of Meaning is also not entirely an explanation of curiosity. The website states

> *Having a purpose and meaning to why each of us on this earth is important to living a life of happiness and fulfilment. Rather than the pursuit of pleasure and material wealth, there is an actual meaning to the PERMA use of meaning – the positive psychology of life. Such meaning gives people a reason for their life and that there is a greater purpose to life.*

This definition hints at the meaning of curiosity in the phrase "a reason for their life". A related phrase used by the positive psychologists is "why each of us is on this earth". But curiosity extends well beyond this question. We are not only curious about why we are on this earth; we are also curious about many other related questions. One that we only partially tackled in an earlier chapter is how we, individually or collectively, or through our governments, can contribute to making ourselves happy - and our fellow citizens.

Curiosity is also not there on the Greek list. The ancient philosophers, however, were themselves curious. The psychologists claim Aristotle was the first psychologist. Many claim he was responsible for the early introduction of the methods of empirical observation in the scientific approach to finding answers to human curiosity. It is a curiosity that drives us all. Phillip, 71, responded to the questionnaire as follows:

> *"YES. In some ways, I am more interested in the world, other people, philosophy, politics, religion, art, etc., than I was when younger. Then I was focused on achieving within my profession. I could argue that this makes being over 70 more fun. There are advantages to aging, and diversity of interest is one".*

Curiosity has to be placed high on the list. The reason is not only that some of the positive psychologists have recommended it. Curiosity signifies that you have an enquiring mind, a mind that has asked itself what is important to you, and where you have also found the reason why that activity is important. And that you have therefore decided to pursue that activity. Also, as we will find, curiosity impinges on the broader issue of how we help each other, individually or collectively through our administrative, social and political systems. It is a question that demands considerable curiosity to even begin the search for an answer.

Curiosity, however, does not fit in readily with all the PERMA acronyms Positive Emotion, Engagement, Relationships, Meaning, Accomplishments. This writer would add a C for curiosity. i.e. a PERMAC.

Positive emotion is a requirement that this research supports. As we found in the various studies, people with a positive outlook on life lead longer and healthier lives. The positive psychology website describes it as:

> *This element of the model is one of the most obvious connections to happiness. Being able to focus on positive emotions is more than just smiling, it is the ability to be optimistic and view the past, present, and future from a positive perspective.*
>
> *This positive view of life can help you in relationships, work, and inspire you to be more creative and take more chances. In everyone's life, there are highs and lows. Focusing on the lows increases your chances of developing depression, therefore, you should focus on the high and positive aspects of life. There are also many health benefits to optimism and positivity.*

The website goes on to state that positive emotion includes "intellectual stimulation and creativity, for example when a child completes a complex lego car that requires his concentration, he will be beaming with joy and satisfaction from his work."

This writer accepts this definition, although with a reservation. That reservation is that if you have positive emotion, one would think you are already there. You are already fulfilled, already happy. There is no need to look for and build your happiness. The Positive Emotion of PERMAC could, therefore, drop the P. The argument for retention, however, is stronger. This author has the suspicion that if you do not have a positive outlook, building up the remainder of the attributes – the ERMAC - will be a near impossible task. Somehow, you need to inculcate in yourself, a positive outlook on life. This writer believes that in the search for other ERMAC attributes, P is a necessary starter.

How then to get to that start point? Just say to yourself, on every issue that you are inclined to complain about, "I am not going to be negative on this issue, I will look for positive ways to handle it. I will just keep trying. And if I cannot find a positive way, I will change it if I can; otherwise, I will try to ignore it". In the many discussions that came up on the frailties of ageing, on the accompanying aches and pains, or even more serious illnesses, this stoic attitude arose: I will live with it, Ignore it to the best of my ability

High on this writer's list is accomplishments. Seligman and his supporters include this attribute. They are telling us here that you need to achieve some successes with your tasks, with your overriding project or projects. I agree with them. It seems to me that if you are succeeding with your projects, you will be happy. Or at least fulfilled. The question then is if you are not accomplishing much, what do you do? The answer lies, it would seem, in three possibilities, to (i) lower your expectations, (ii) change your project, or (iii) just keep striving. This writer favours the third. It is seen in the often-quoted sayings:" If at first, you do not succeed, try again," or "Nothing ventured, nothing gained". Both proverbs have been with us for a long time. The first is of nineteenth century origin in English storytelling but the second is worldwide, appearing to have come from a thirteenth century Icelandic saga. It would seem that accomplishment itself is a desirable goal, but that it is not the ultimate goal. The happiness, the fulfilment is in the striving. Yours may not be the most effective men's' shed in the neighbourhood, but your joy, your fulfilment comes through your efforts to make it so.

Virtue, although not part of PERMAC, does intrude. It was Aristotle's requirement. He, and several of the later positive psychologists, required it in some form. This writer also believes that virtue, in some form, is necessary for a happy life. Its requirement is for us to lead a good life, an ethical life. At its simplest, it is based on the belief, mentioned above, that people who harm others, who steal from them, who lie to them or assault them, are not happy. In the examination of the role of government in Chapter 9 in contributing to a happy life (and in the Afterword), the requirement of exercising virtue emerged as a requirement on us to minimise the difficulties, the harm that others experience. It is an obligation on us all. Virtue is not clearly defined. David Hume, an 18th.Century British philosopher, listed over 70 virtues. [1] Virtue is still a difficult attribute to define. The afterword has attempted to provide a definition that is simpler, and more universal and useful. This definition is that our overriding moral obligation is not to harm people and to help those who need help.

If we adopt this requirement of virtue, the acronym becomes VPERMAC. From many discussions, and from the survey, together with the early Greek commitment to virtue, it appears that some form of volunteering is high, although not the highest on peoples' lists. In fact, the questionnaire results place it only in ninth position. But volunteering is only one avenue for expressing virtue. As noted above, learning or curiosity along with our contributions to the thinking of our governments could be others.

Equally high in the answers from all three sources, the early philosophers, the modern psychologists, and the over 65 respondents, is engagement. The positive psychologists describe it as identifying your strengths and developing a plan to implement them into your life. Character strengths form a large part of engagement and of your project, or projects, i.e. that activity or activities which occupy a large segment of your attention and time.

Other findings from the survey that are of great interest and correlate well with the psychologists and the early Greek philosophers are good friends and close relationships. They are one theme that comes through in all sources, scoring well across all findings. Closeness with your partner, even the joy of grandchildren, comes through in the survey findings. But it is not at all clear how one achieves friendships or even ensures closeness with your partner.

Aristotle wrote extensively on friendship, but he did exhibit some tendency for using friends for his own benefit, as did the twentieth century's recommendation by Dale Carnegie, as discussed in an earlier chapter. One might like someone because he/she is useful, or because they are pleasant, Aristotle tells us. This writer believes that a genuine joy in the companionship and thoughts of another, accompanied by a desire to seek that companionship, continuing over the years, is the underlying basis of a good friendship. Cicero also wrote on friendship, defining it as complete sympathy in all matters of importance, plus goodwill and affection[2]. Without these virtues, friendship cannot exist.

The question of a partner in life also appears to influence one's happiness, a finding that comes through most of all in the survey results, and on which some respondents wrote at length. It is an issue that this writer is very hesitant to provide his thoughts, fully aware that his thoughts contain no more expertise and knowledge than that of anyone else. It is perhaps preferable to present the statements of one 82-year-old respondent, Richard. It was clear that he and his partner put much effort into enjoying the other's company, but it was not effort in terms of work effort, but effort in the sense of encouraging and boosting the togetherness and fulfilment of their relationship. They frequently toasted "to us"; to themselves. It seems, however, that it would require both of you to work at encouraging this sense of a pair, this togetherness. One person cannot do it alone. It requires both people to make the effort. The benefits of a togetherness in life would seem to be worth the effort involved. Even the effort in continuing when the other partner is not fully supportive. That raises the question then if the other really does not want to work at the togetherness, what to do about it? This author's answer is the same as that given above for the project in your life. Find a new one.

Finally, one answer that partially comes through in the survey, and in the readings, is the need for financial security. Aristotle said it; the psychologists say it, albeit only indirectly; and it is equal fourth with leisure on the questionnaire answers. This study did attempt to relate unhappiness with poverty through the questionnaire. The question was asked whether the survey respondents considered themselves relatively well off or not. Virtually all respondents put themselves in the middle of the income range, neither rich nor poor. Hopefully, it is a finding that will become clearer in the ongoing research for future editions of this book.

The assumption has been made, however, that poverty does not auger well for a happy life. That assumption brings with it a particular inference: that if Plato, Aristotle and Cicero, along with several of the positive psychologists are correct, in that we need to have at least some sufficiency of the world's goods, then one role of government is to ensure that every attempt be made to eliminate poverty. The differing persuasions of our various governments, however, who are still arguing over this task, make it unlikely that the problem of poverty will be solved soon. The upset election of Donald Trump by a majority of working class whites, who believe that they have been going backwards economically, along with the huge and growing disparities in income and wealth in most developed countries, is evidence of the inadequacies of government policies. They also create difficulties in ensuring that we all are reasonably well off when we quit work.

In 2016 Oxfam published a study concluding that the world's richest 62 people own as much wealth as the poorest half of the world population[3]. That is, 53 men and nine women have the same amount of money and assets as 3.6 billion people have collectively. But in January 2017 Oxfam published a correction. New data showed that the richest eight people last year had the same wealth as the poorest 3.6 billion[4].

For readers in the industrialised countries of the West, the requirement that we need "sufficient of the worlds goods" for a happy life after 65, does suggest that we need to start early on the task of ensuring that we are at least comfortable when we reach that age. This book is not an exercise in wealth creation, but readers still in mid-life are well advised to consult one or more of the many wealth accumulation books or websites that are available. One of the most useful pieces of advice that this author has come across is that just $6 a day invested at 8 per cent from age 20 will make you a millionaire at 65. Better still, only about $100,000 will have come out of your pocket; nearly $900,000 will be "free" investment returns. The injunction to start early includes assuring ourselves that we are protected and housed if we succumb to one of the afflictions of old age That we do not leave these vital decisions to our partners or our children.

But if we stay healthy, and live longer, and that we have the means to support the curiosity, we also need to find activities that 'turn us on' as we get older.

Those projects, those activities that turn us on, would also not appear to have any need to be intellectual. As mentioned it could be starting up and running the local men's shed. But, on all projects, to obtain maximum satisfaction, a full commitment and some degree of achievement would be required.

The demands on Governments

This is an issue into which all people, but particularly those over 65, for they have the time, should put some effort. This issue has been discussed in the previous chapter. The writer's priorities, and the priorities we should place on our governments, are shown in Figure 10.1.

Figure 10.1
The Author's Priorities

1. Understanding the world better. What makes people behave badly, or well. Whether it is genetically inherited from our distant past or acquired; and what we can do about the less acceptable attributes.
2. Updating this book (on happiness in older people), by extending the research to include more countries and a wider spread of replies from those who are less well-off.
3. Providing support for the disadvantaged; and for the elimination of poverty
4. Determining universal and identifiable guidelines on moral wrongdoing.
5. (and strengthening the willingness to expose that wrongdoing),
6. Stopping war… by strengthening the United Nations as a world policeman.
7. Strengthening the analytical and thinking ability of the educated elites.

8. Making all governments responsive to the wishes of their people.
9. Caring for and housing refugees, in Australia and world-wide
10. Outlawing the death penalty everywhere.

This listing appears to ignore the priorities of the developing nations, which as you will remember, were jobs and food. This listing, however, does require more responsive government. The answers to the jobs and food issues also lie in effective government. Millions have been brought out of poverty in South East Asia through effective government policies.[5]

But the highest priority on this list is a desire to do something positive about the world's less attractive attributes. The following Afterword is the approach proposed by this author to create that better world. It is not a proposal put forward by any of the contributors to this book – the early philosophers, the responders to the questionnaire, of the positive psychologists of the 21st century. That is why it has been set out in an Afterword. But, if adopted, it is the author's belief that it will make the world a happier place.

AFTERWORD

This book has documented some of the many observations on happiness over the centuries, ranging from the earliest philosophers, several centuries before the Christian era, to the recommendations of modern psychologists. Along with these findings were the results of a questionnaire to 150 or more people over 65. Among the many findings were the recommendations on virtue as a path to happiness. Aristotle, in his book, *Nicomachean Ethics*, linked virtue with eudaimonia, his word for happiness or a fulfilling life. Cicero gave him total support. The twentieth century positive psychologists also clearly advocate virtue as a way to a happy life. Even some of the over 65 survey respondents advocated a virtuous life (although it must be admitted, their aggregated response was not all that enthusiastic). Plato also argues that we should refrain from harming others, as to do so is a virtue. His argument is found, among other sources, in his dialogue Meno. Socrates asserts that virtues are common to all people, that temperance (exercising self-control) and justice (fairness with other people) are virtues, even in children and old men. For Plato's mouthpiece, Socrates, justice is clearly a major virtue, and virtuous actions clearly cannot harm others. Research by Steven Delue and Timothy Dale gives this statement a 21st century philosophical endorsement. Their book is on the political structure and management of society. It is relatively easy to accept the concept that if the world was virtuous, we would all be happier. We may not be able to prevent sickness and ill-health, but we would not have to endure the harms inflicted on us by lies, thefts, assaults, even war.

Then what is virtue? There are multiple definitions. Is it all the virtues listed by David Hume, an 18th century philosopher, in *An Enquiry Concerning the Principles of Morals*, and other works, who put forward around seventy virtues?[1] Is it the 24 character strengths and virtues developed by the modern positive psychologists, and set out in an earlier chapter? Alasdair MacIntyre, in *After Virtue* covers the many virtues that appeared in Homer, in the New Testament, Thomas Aquinas, Benjamin Franklin, and in Jane Austin. Do we need all the virtues? If not, which are the ones that bring us happiness?

If we use the moral theories that have been developed over the years - the theories for defining whether actions are right or wrong - as our method of defining virtue, we find that there are over 20 of them. One of the subsets of these theories is Virtue Ethics. According to one of its principal supporters (Julia Annas[2]), it would have about seven versions.

This afterword, therefore, attempts to define virtue. If a considerable body of learned opinion over the centuries tells us that virtue is necessary for happiness, then it is highly desirable that we determine what it is. This Afterword puts forward the thesis that all the virtues can be subsumed into one overall rule. That virtuous behaviour is captured by the phrase "Help others, or at least do not harm them". Embedded in this thesis is the obligation that if people are already suffering under some harm, we are obliged to help them as best we can.

The following paragraphs outline the reasons why this author advocates the "Do no harm" rule as the definition of virtue - as the one universal overriding moral doctrine. Those who find moral philosophical arguments tedious, or who accept the universality of "Do no harm" can skip the following sections and go straight to the final sections, one asserting that this rule will be observed more thoroughly than any of the current moral rules. There is also a final section on the application of the 'Do no harm' rule". That section applies the do no harm rule to the ethical and moral concerns of today's world. The reasons for including the intervening paragraphs is that they portray moral philosophy as an unthinking practice. Philosophers will disagree. Hence a solid case needs to be made.

These intervening sections cover

(i) The many current moral issues and arguments that exist in the world now. How to resolve them is a problem.
(ii) The twenty or more current moral theories that do not give us any help. In fact, they provide us with methods to support opposing sides of various moral disagreements.
(iii) The reason for these opposing opinions is that moral philosophers base their thinking on argument. It is a totally inadequate method for reaching a decision.
(iv) These sections also outline the methods that were used to search for a universal moral guideline.
(v) If we are looking for a fundamental moral rule to guide the world, the "Do no harm" rule encapsulates, even improves on John Rawls' widely endorsed "veil of ignorance".
(vi) The universality of the 'Do no harm' rule is evidenced by the social improvements over recent centuries.

The final section concludes by applying the do no harm rule to the more common of today's moral controversies.

(i) The world has many current moral issues

Whether the US should have launched 60 cruise missiles against the Syrian Air force base is one of several such issues. Banning Muslim immigration or threatening to build a wall to keep out Mexicans are two more controversial issues.

Even our smaller controversies of virtue are numerous: an unwillingness to further liberalise our treatment of gays to embrace same sex marriage, the escalating differentiation between rich and poor, a refusal to adopt gun control in the United States, the abolition of sections of the Racial Discrimination Act in Australia, and the vote for Brexit in the UK are examples. We have differences of opinion everywhere: Euthanasia, our responses to refugees, collateral damage, human induced global warming, abortion, designer babies, capital punishment, are additional examples of controversial issues. Millions of people advocate one side or the other on these issues. We have no universal moral guideline. After 2000 years of moral philosophising we still do not have an agreed method of distinguishing between right action and that which is wrong. Or unacceptable.

(ii) The current moral theories do not provide a guideline

One of the reasons is that we do not know the differences between right and wrong is the multitude of moral guidelines that have been developed. It is incredible, even unbelievable, that after years of argument, moral philosophers are still disagreeing on what is the virtuous action, and what is a morally wrong action.

Over the centuries, philosophers have developed twenty or more moral theories.

The more common moral theories are (i) Immanuel Kant's deontology, which has at least three versions, including his first formulation: "Act only on that maxim through which you can at the same time will that it (your action) should become a universal law." (ii) Utilitarianism (or consequentialism) which has four – Jeremy Bentham's, John Stuart Mill's, Peter Singer's and act and rule utilitarianism, and (iii) Virtue which, as mentioned, has at least seven. There are three additional moral pluralist theories – Frankena's, Gert's, and Beauchamp and Childress's. A quick search on the internet will reveal at least seven more – moral subjectiveness (what you 'feel' is right), cultural relativism, ethical egoism, divine command theory, rights-based theories, justice as fairness, and stoic virtue. This listing does not include the ethical theories of the Continental (except for Kant) or Asian philosophers, or feminist or race ethics.

My underlying concern is that these competing theories do not tell us how to behave in morally conflicting situations. Some big issues, murder, robbery, physical assault, for example, are clear. They are against the law. But others, perhaps even bigger, are disputed. This multitude of ethical theories allows you, the observer, when faced with an ethical choice, to choose different responses to an ethical problem. First, Kant's formulation: "Act only on that maxim through which you can at the same time will that it (your action) should become a universal law" enables those on either side of these current debates to convince themselves that their position is the universal law (and should be accepted by others as such). In short, Kant's imperative allows us to choose opposing or conflicting solutions to a current issue.

A second reason why the guidelines are ineffective is that they frequently call for a neutral observer. Adam Smith and David Hume espoused early versions of this ideal observer theory. I suggest that those on either side of the above issues readily believe that that they are impartial observers. It is the opposing viewpoint that is biased.

The current moral rules are, therefore, ineffective in resolving the numerous world-wide ethical problems that we argue about today.

These current issues are ethical questions. They relate to the well-being of particular groups in society, or in some cases, our entire society. That association classifies the issues as ethical. Each of the issues listed above can be answered by the thesis of this Afterword– that doing no harm to others or helping others is a dominant or overriding ethical guideline.

Our beliefs on the evolution of morality also reflect our basic human natures. There are numerous texts which argue that our moral instincts are evolved. *What Makes Us Moral* [3] and *The Evolution of Morality* [4] are two among many. The thesis that our moral instincts are a result of our evolutionary history is supported by the evidence that the world has experienced a huge strengthening in moral practices over the centuries. See Stephen Pinker's *The Better Angels of Our Nature,* or his later book *Enlightenment Now* Both are persuasive documentations of the strengthening of our social practices in recent centuries.

An appeal to common sense concepts of virtue does not help either. The reason here is that some virtues give a two-sided answer. If the Gestapo come looking for Jewish families in the neighbourhood, do you tell them the truth? - that you have such a family hidden in your attic. Another example of people on either side of the current debates being convinced that theirs is the virtuous position is the churches on same sex marriage. Many religious people are also against abortion. It could be expected that they would take what they consider to be a virtuous position, but as evidenced below, same sex marriage may break a religious ruling, but it breaks no moral law.

(iii) The current moral guidelines are based on argument

The underlying reason behind this conflict is that philosophical thought is based on argument. The Philosopher's Blog has its definition of argument as a set of claims:

> *While people generally think of an argument as a fight, this is not the case - at least as the term is used in philosophy. In philosophy, an argument is a set of claims, any one of which is supposed to set out the philosophical position that the reader should adopt.*

There would not be a philosophy department world-wide that does not make the claim that argument is its preferred method of reaching a philosophical decision. It is a questionable method, as the practice in the profession is to retain all the arguments, i.e., not to reach a decision. The net effect has been to create the twenty or more claims for different ethical guidelines. The poor student of philosophy must not only learn these moral theories, but the multitude of other philosophical arguments that have been thrown up.

Virtually every other discipline must reach a solution – a business cannot live with multiple arguments or solutions to its decisions on pricing, distribution systems, etc. - it must decide. Governments may have multiple options, but if the problem is pressing enough, they will be forced to decide. The sciences also may have multiple theories. But again, we know that all sides are working towards finding an answer. Even if the different opinion be on the origins of the universe, or the existence of life on other planets, or the evolution of Homo floresiensis, we are sure that one day, we will get an agreed solution.

Not so moral philosophy. The position of this Afterword is that the current issues under debate globally are fundamentally ethical questions; that we need to decide, in the interests of those faced with these choices, which position is ethically the more desirable. The world would benefit immeasurably if we agreed on one overriding ethical guideline. This guideline suggested in this Afterword is not to harm others. And if they are suffering harm, to help alleviate that harm in any way we see fit.

(iv) The Search for a universal moral guideline

The search started for this writer during the years spent teaching ethics. The initial research method was to search out difficult moral questions and apply the main theories - deontology and utilitarianism – to see if they gave a useful answer. The answers initially tended towards John Stuart Mill's *Utilitarianism*, primarily due to its "Do no harm" component. Further research identified three additional theories with a "do no harm component ". These Western theories were Beauchamp and Childress's *Principles of Biomedical Ethics*, William Frankena's *Ethics*, Bernard Gert's *Common Morality* along with John Stuart Mill's *Utilitarianism*.

During this process, the realisation came that the theories all originated in Western philosophy. A lengthy search through the Eastern religions identified an overwhelming support for a "Do no harm" rule: *Ahimsa*

Each of these theories- Western as well as Eastern - is examined below to determine how well it addresses the moral issues outlined above. Included in this analysis are concerns of defining harm; along with the theory's effectiveness in balancing harms. e.g., in weighing a small harm against the prevention of a larger one; and whether it incorporates the relieving of harm already incurred. i.e., a "Do good" as well as a "Do not do harm" injunction.

Beauchamp and Childress: Principles of Biomedical Ethics: Their work is a bio-ethics text, but it can double as a general ethics text. It specifies four separate principles that structure the authors' theory - respect for autonomy, non-maleficence, beneficence and justice.

Non- maleficence is the do no harm component. Beauchamp and Childress (B&C) also specify beneficence, which is their answer to the question of whether we are supposed to do good or not. They lead their readers somewhat along the decision path of where we should do good, by specifying "where", "when", "who" and "how" – (pp. 379-81). For example, Peter Singer's case of rescuing a drowning child where the only risk to the rescuer is dirtying his/her clothes, sets out the concept that we have an obligation to remedy harm suffered by others.

B&C also argue respect for autonomy.

B&C's guidelines cover three ethical obligations, including suffering harm in order to do a greater good. But they are set out in a medical context. The justice issues are treated in this same context. Issues of justice in the world at large are not their concern.

William Frankena: His 1973 book *Ethics* possibly covers much of what we are looking for as any of the theories. It has a four-part set of rules:

1. One ought not to inflict evil or harm.
2. One ought to prevent evil or harm - includes injuries, interferences and deceit.
3. One ought to remove evil. Includes removing existing injuries and harms
4. One ought to do or promote good by making others happy; by improving their well-being.

Frankena adds several amplifications: One ought to make some contribution to the goodness of others' lives; ensuring equality of opportunity; of access to education and justice before the law. He also adds that we should not lie.

He has set out a comprehensive program. He clearly states that we should attempt to correct for harm already suffered. He does not appear to provide a guideline, however, on balancing one harm against another - the extent to which we should accept a smaller harm in order to prevent a larger wrong. Nor again does he cover issues such as increasing disparity of wealth and incomes in the world. In addition, his work is almost a half century old, and does not appear to have captured the world's attention in the same way the theories of John Stuart Mill or Bernard Gert have done.

Bernard Gert: *Common Morality.* Gert's ten rules of common morality are

1. Do not kill
2. Do not cause pain
3. Do not disable
4. Do not deprive of freedom
5. Do not deprive of pleasure
6. Do not deceive
7. Keep your promises
8. Do not cheat
9. Obey the law
10. Do your duty

A two-step process of moral decision is suggested (pp. 58-79). In the first step, a moral decision-maker works out whether an action would be a violation of one of the ten moral rules. If it would not, then the act is justified. If not permissible, the second step requires an estimation of the consequences of the violation. A balance of the estimated benefits over harms then informs the decision maker whether this violation of the moral rules is justifiable.

Gert then raises some of the questions outlined earlier - how we define harm; can we inflict a small harm in order to prevent a larger one? And whether we are obliged to relieve a harm already suffered by another? He does say that we should balance harms. Unfortunately, he does not give us guidelines that are clear or precise enough to tell us how we could balance one harm against another.

Also, his "Obey the Law" rule faces the problem that not all laws are just, or even ethical. Several countries, for instance, have laws where you are not allowed to criticise those who hold power - North Korea, Eritrea, Cuba, Uzbekistan, and Belarus, for instance. Turkey is also now seeing an increasing totalitarianism with 81 journalists in jail according to the Committee to Protect Journalists. We could question Gert's requirement to "Obey the law" in these countries.

Gert's requirement to obey the law has validity, however, in that the whistle-blower protection laws that have now been introduced in over 70 countries worldwide. They usually provide protection for whistle-blowers who expose the contravening of an existing law. Whistle-blower legislation in the United States is slightly different to that available in the other countries. The US specifies that protection is available under each individual law, some 65 in total. The US system makes the task of the whistle-blower much more difficult. It is simpler to make an overall guideline "Obey the Law."

John Stuart Mill's *Utilitarianism* is clearly against harming others. He repeats this injunction several times:

- The moral rules which forbid mankind to hurt one another... are more vital to human well-being than any maxims, however important, which only point out the best mode of managing some department of human affairs. (*Utilitarianism*, Chapter 5, para 31).
- A person may possibly not need the benefits of others; but he always needs that they should not do him hurt. (Ch. 5, para 31).
- (U)tility includes not solely the pursuit of happiness, but the prevention or mitigation of unhappiness (Ch.2, para 13).

Mill also promotes happiness. He describes utility as the "Greatest Happiness Principle".

> The creed which accepts as the foundation of morals, Utility, or the Greatest Happiness Principle, holds that actions are right in propor-

tion as they tend to promote happiness, wrong as they tend to produce the reverse of happiness.

Mill also uses the word pain in a very wide sense, although perhaps not always clearly. In its common usage, the word describes a physical pain in parts of the body. Mill clearly used it in a wider sense, for he offers the term "deprivation of pleasure" as an alternative. He also includes "mental suffering" as one of the contributors to unhappiness.

Mill offers strong support for personal autonomy in his *On Liberty*. Accepting these definitions as the guidelines from Mill's theories we find a strong injunction against harming others together with the objective of promoting peoples' happiness.

Ahimsa or "Do no harm" has the support of the Asian philosophies. The twenty or so competing theories are all drawn from Western philosophy, primarily from the English-speaking nations. This writer had the good fortune to spend some time in Asian countries, sufficient to learn that Buddhism, Jainism, even Islam, also had moral thoughts to offer the Western world. In the multitude of messages of sympathy that were broadcast after the Nice terrorist attack was a repeat of the pronouncement by Tenzin Gyatso, the 14th Dalai Lama: "Our prime purpose in life is to help others. And if you cannot help them, at least don't hurt them". In the Hindu, Buddhist, and Jain philosophies is the concept of ahimsa: "Respect for All Living Things and Avoidance of Violence Towards Others". Non-violence, as we are all aware, is "at the core of Mahatma Gandhi's political thought".[5]

Debrata Sen Sharma, writing on Hindu ethics, claims that Hindu, Buddhist and Jain thinkers advocate that we should "abstain… from violence in any form and refrain from causing injury to any one through deed, word or thought". This injunction may require some effort to observe. The US Supreme Court has repeatedly ruled that hate speech, no matter how bigoted or offensive, is free speech.

The Samyoga Institute tells us: "Although ahimsa was originally translated as non-killing, it evolved over time to mean non-injury- physically, mentally and/or verbally." This interpretation suggests that we not strike anyone, make unpleasant statements, or even think negative thoughts about people we know.

The classical Hippocratic Oath is at least partial support for the "Do no harm" guideline. Uncertain in origin, it emerged maybe a century after Hippocrates: "I will keep them (the sick) from harm and injustice".

Even Islam, a religion currently under considerable fire, puts forward a theory which supports the thesis of this Afterword. Hazrat Mirza Tahir Ahmad, Head of the Ahmadiyya Movement in Islam, in a 1992 speech available on its website, Al Islam, summarises a host of rules that flow from the fundamentals in the Quran about any system of government: These rules are, in effect, a "Do no harm, care for others" rule. (The numbers in brackets are references to the appropriate verses in the Quran):

- A government is duty-bound to protect the honour, life and property of its people [18].
- A ruler must always act with justice, between individuals and between people [19].
- National matters should be settled by consultation [20].
- Government must arrange to fulfil the basic needs of man: provide him food, clothing and shelter [21].
- People should be provided a peaceful and secure environment, and their lives, property and honour protected [22].
- The economic system should be equitable and orderly [22].
- Health care should be organised [22].
- There should prevail total religious freedom [23].
- A vanquished people must be dealt with justly [24].
- Prisoners of war should be treated with compassion [25].
- Treaties and agreements must always be honoured [26].
- Iniquitous agreements must not be forced upon the weak [26].
- Muslim subjects are enjoined to obey the government in authority. The only exception to this rule is a case where the government blatantly opposes and prevents the carrying out of religious duties and obligations [27]

Abū Ḥāmid Muḥammad al-Ghazālī (1058 –1111) was a Muslim philosopher and mystic from Persia. Ghazali wrote *The Alchemy of Happiness*. It was a rewrite of *The Revival of Religious Sciences* republished under a new name. Al-Ghazali emphasized that only a few have attained supreme happiness, which is culminated in a union with the divine. These few were the prophets. *The Revival of Religious Sciences* is a long book, possibly the most read after the Qur'an in the Muslim world. As a book on Muslim spirituality, it was thought to preclude Al- Ghazali from the cross-section of writers on happiness documented in an earlier chapter.

Another support for the "Do No harm, help others" guideline is the two forms of the Golden rule: "Do not do to others as you would not wish done to you". and "Do unto others…" It is a rule endorsed by all churches and religions.

(v) John Rawls' veil of ignorance

This search for a universal moral guideline started with "Do no harm". There were several reasons why. Initially, it was by asking what is the most basic ethical responsibility that we should demonstrate to other people. My answer then was that it is to do them no harm. At an even higher conceptual level, this theory is extended for people are already suffering a harm - that we should alleviate that harm as best we can. An initial reading of John Stuart Mill's *Utilitarianism*, and particularly his much-repeated injunction that happiness is achieved by not harming others, was the impetus. His opening sentences about the then existing philosophical conflicts warned that there was little agreement on this topic:

> *From the dawn of philosophy, the question concerning the summum bonum, or, what is the same thing, concerning the foundation of morality, has been accounted the main problem in speculative thought, has occupied the most gifted intellects, and divided them into sects and schools, carrying on a vigorous warfare against one another.*

Then came John Rawls, *a Theory of Justice*, and his Veil of Ignorance. Rawls proposes that behind this veil, you know nothing of yourself and your natural abilities, or your position in society. You know nothing of your sex, race, nationality, or individual tastes, but you decide the type of world you want to end up in. His thought experiment is brilliant and certainly would result in us designing a very just and equitable world. But Rawls attacks utilitarianism almost on every page, claiming that he, Rawls, wants his theory to supplant utility. It was a claim that bewildered this reader, for he thought that Rawls' *Theory of Justice* and Mill's *Utilitarianism* would have the same impact. In short, the implementation of Rawls or Mill would end with similar worlds.

We can play another thought experiment. This time the magic fairy appears, offering you the chance to return in the next round to a world in which you can change just one aspect of human behaviour. What would be your choice? It might be a world without war, the ending of the grab for power, or a world with honest political leaders. One respondent, in the many conversations about these findings, answered the abolition of envy. The answer of this author is that we want a world in which we universally would help others, and above all, do them no harm.

(vi) The human race has unwittingly adopted 'Do no harm'

No harm to others/ do good has further support in that it has been behind the social movements of history – the abolition of slavery, the ending of feudalism, the rise of participative government, the creation of the welfare state and the provision of sickness, disability and old age benefits. Anyone who has witnessed the unbelievable sadness faced by an unmarried mother whose child has been taken away from her at birth will see the provision of support for single mothers in a very positive light. A dominant lesson that has emerged from history is also that we should extend the benefit we have awarded to one particular group to all other groups. To continue to discriminate against groups such as women, gays, black communities, refugees, etc. is to harm them.

The ending of colonialism and the growth of universal suffrage in the developing world is yet another major social improvement. And then there was the ending of child labour. As Bertrand Russell put it: "Child labour in England was developed to a point of appalling cruelty" [6].

The above listing of social improvements to date further demonstrate that the world has, in effect, adopted this guideline over many years. There is no reason why the impact of our sentiments and feelings for people suffering a harm would not continue to widen and develop further in future years.

Will this rule be observed?

A further question arises then, is if we reduce the 15 - 20 theories to just this one, will it have any impact? This Afterword argues yes. More people will listen, be more inclined to obey that rule. Those on the winning side of the ethical disagreements enumerated above, will be able to make the claim, with greater validity, that theirs is the position that should be universally accepted. In short, worldwide moral opinion will be on the side of those who argue against harming, for helping others.

The do no harm rule is supported by basic human emotions Breakey, in discussing moral pluralism, argues that "There is substantial psychological and anthropological evidence that human beings do draw upon distinct and irreducible moral principles when they are thinking and acting ethically," [7] quoting Nichols and Gill [8] as well as Gibbs [9]. These and many other theorists argue that our morality is based on natural human sentiments – sentiments that come into play when we feel that another person is wronged or harmed. Coplan and Goldie, also Killen & Smetana, [10] argue that empathy with and for others is our basic human emotion. The huge outpouring of world support for people in poorer countries afflicted by natural disasters, or by war, is further evidence of this human emotion.

The "do no harm" rule, when adopted, will also be taught in schools. Currently, ethics classes in schools teach philosophical ethics. That version, as does philosophy generally, relies on argument. If you have a good convincing argument, then what every action or position that you adopt, you can claim to be ethical. The "Do no harm" rule will facilitate resolution of most ethical disagreements. This resolution will be worldwide, thus making it much more difficult for an unethical solution to be adopted.

A final argument for adopting the "Do no harm, help others" as the embodiment of a virtuous life in John Locke's *Essays on the Law of Nature* (1664), an early work That expressed a position from which he never diverted:

> *since man has been made such as he is, equipped with reason and his other faculties and destined for this mode of life, there necessarily result from his inborn constitution some definite duties for him, which cannot be other than they are.*

The Encyclopaedia Britannica interprets this statement as "Just as one can discover from the nature of the triangle that its angles equal two right angles, so this moral order can be discovered by reason and is within the grasp of all human beings." In this author's words. The Do no harm; Help others rule in just common sense

Although widespread acceptance of the "Do no harm" rule will assist in resolving the currently debated ethical issues, it is still not a universal answer. There is one activity of the human race which has caused unbelievable suffering – war. Deaths in WWII are estimated at between 50 and 80 million. We see the misery of the current warfare in Syria on our TV screens every night. A quarter of a million Syrians have been killed and over one million injured. 4.8 million Syrians have been forced to leave their country, and 6.5 million are internally displaced. The moral belief that we should not harm others will not resolve the issue of war. We need to find other methods. That will require research into our international political options. It is this author's belief that war is primarily caused by a country, through its leaders, wishing to take over the land or the people of another country. Emperors and the like, from Alexander, the Roman Emperors, Napoleon, through to Hitler, are evidence.

War is perhaps the biggest moral issue that the world faces. Clearly war is against the "Do no harm rule." But the existence of the rule will not stop war. The world has no universal policeman. Whether the countries that make up the United Nations can be persuaded to give up any of their autonomy – at minimum to install some type of policing function – is questionable. Exploring ways in which they may be persuaded is a step towards further universalising the do no harm rule. How we stop them is a question for some 65 plus researcher. But the rule makes us pacifists. If the world can establish a universal policeman, that policeman at times must go to war to prevent a larger war. Such a policeman would have been fully justified in preventing Saddam Hussein's invasion of Kuwait. But would it have been justified in invading Iraq? Preventive strikes, no matter how powerful the incentive, are also questionable, for they cause harm. Two of the most notorious in history – the German invasion of Belgium in WWI or Israel's preventive strike in the 1967 Six-day war, are, under this rule, morally debatable.

Perhaps as important a question as those above is whether "Do no harm" also does require us to make what efforts we can to relieve the harm already suffered by another. A "Do no harm" injunction, when augmented with a "Do good" imperative, raises still further questions. One such question is the issue of justice, and the massive imbalances in the wealth and income in the world, and the question of how do we address those issues. This is also an issue for further research.

Applying the Do no harm guideline

The "Do no harm" rule, however, faces problems. First is how do we define harm? Is giving offence, for instance, harming someone? Also, can we inflict a small harm to prevent a larger one? This issue is the same question as the search for an answer to the trolley problem and similar issues.[11]. Can we kill one to save five? A real-life equivalent is the question of collateral damage. Is the killing of innocent bystanders morally permissible even if we inflict much greater damage to our enemies?

Deciding what is harm can be difficult. The 22-year-old male peeping through the window at a female neighbour undressing is doing no harm. But it is clearly unacceptable. But the action raises yet another issue – is intruding on a person's privacy doing them harm? The requirement to respect another's privacy clearly came from the Kantian imperative to never treat humans as a means to an end. It is a central value in the Kantian tradition of moral philosophy. The issue of a person's autonomy was also of concern to J.S. Mill. It is given a fundamental status in Mill's version of utilitarian liberalism. The Stanford Encyclopedia of Philosophy states that autonomy is leading one's life according to reasons and motives that are one's own and not the product of manipulative or distorting external forces. The Peeping Tom, therefore, is breaking the" no- harm rule".

Can we commit harm if we believe our action is in the interests of the wider community? Mill in *On Liberty*, argued that "The only purpose for which power can be rightfully exercised over any member of a civilized community, against his will, is to prevent harm to others." France's Declaration of the Rights of Man and of the Citizen of 1789 also stated: "Liberty consists in the freedom to do everything which injures no one else." The answer would appear to be that we weigh the harms, one against the other, and decide. But as will be seen below, we need to develop research methods which more fully enable us to answer this question.

The position of this author is that do no harm to others is an absolute rule. The movie *Eye in the Sky* with Helen Mirren as Colonel Katherine Powell gives us an example. She must decide, along with senior military officers and politicians, up to the level of the British Prime Minister, whether to launch a guided missile on a house with two already loaded suicide bombers about to leave. The collateral damage is a street vendor outside who would be killed if a drone strike is launched. Colonel Powell does launch the drone. If no harm to others is an absolute imperative, then we do not launch the drone. The suicide bombers are free to kill many others.

Many observers would disagree with the guideline that we do not kill the suicide bombers. Two counter-arguments to this position can be identified: One is that we – the liberal democracies - are supposed to be on the side of right. We are leading the world to a higher moral level. The practices and beliefs of the democracies establish a universal guideline for humanity. We do not kill innocent people. Second is that if we adopt a "Do no harm" guideline, then we do not harm anybody. From a similar reasoning, we do not flick the switch to kill one to save five on a runaway trolley. We also see the verification of this belief in the common opinion that we do not push the heavy man off the bridge to derail the runaway trolley. That is deliberate murder.

A recent World Bank research paper indicates that moral appeals do produce results. An Islamic Bank in Indonesia sent out moral appeals to credit card customers about increased credit card repayments. All the bank's late-paying credit card customers received a basic reminder to meet their required minimum payment. Clients in the treatment group also received a text message citing an Islamic religious text that states, "non-repayment of debts by someone who is able to repay is an injustice". This message increased the share of customers meeting their minimum payments by nearly 20 percent. The researchers found that removing religious references from the quote does not change its effectiveness, suggesting that the moral appeal of the message itself, rather than its religious connotation, increased payment [12]

The current moral arguments listed earlier- same sex marriage, the escalating differentiation between rich and poor, a refusal to adopt gun control in the United States, etc. are amenable to the do no harm guideline. Possibly the issues that will be the most disputed will be the bio-ethic issues: abortion, stem cell research, and euthanasia. But if we ask why it is wrong to kill and accepting that it is not yet proven that we were created in God's image, we can only come up with Peter Singer's thesis. It is wrong to kill because we deprive that person of the enjoyment of their future life. Under this thesis, an embryo has no concept of a future life. Using embryos for research, therefore, has no moral implications. In addition, a terminally ill person who does not want the pain of the next few years, is, under that thesis, fully entitled, under safeguards, to give away their life.

More investigation is needed on some of these issues – collateral damage in warfare has been mentioned. Warfare itself is another. Inequity in incomes or in the accumulation of wealth are yet further examples. Moral philosophers have published some cogent arguments based around the principle that if I work harder and smarter than other people, and earn more money, then it is theft to tax me at a higher rate than those other people. For instance, Robert Nozick makes this statement in *Anarchy, State, and Utopia*. It won the 1975 U.S. National Book Award in the Philosophy and Religion category. Translated into 11 languages, it was named one of the "100 most influential books since the war" by the U.K. Times Literary Supplement[13]. But is this higher tax rate theft? Or will "Minimize harm" give us the answer to creating a just society?

The rule also encompasses the possibility of inflicting harm indirectly. An advertisement that is dishonest, even though nobody pays any attention to it, is still immoral. Carelessness, when it opens the possibility of harm is likewise contrary to the do no harm rule. An engineer who does not check her designs is likewise immoral. The collapse of the Westgate bridge in Melbourne which killed 35 workmen, or of the Hyatt Kansas City staircase, which killed 140 guests, were caused by faulty, but unchecked designs. Similar lack of care in the operating theatre can cause harm. Not ensuring that we avoid the possibility of harm is therefore immoral.

The world is facing many moral difficulties at the moment. As a leader in the New York Times said recently (April 21, 2017):[14]

> *The world seems awash in chaos and uncertainty, perhaps more so than at any point since the end of the Cold War. Authoritarian-leaning leaders are on the rise, and liberal democracy itself*

seems under siege. The post-World War II order is fraying as fighting spills across borders and international institutions

The "do no harm" rule will take us a long way towards building a more moral, a more virtuous and happier world. But it will not take us the whole way. Strengthening of our international institutions for the purpose of reducing, if not stopping wars completely, are one set of steps on which we still must agree. Others are the issues referred to by the New York Times, and above all, the conflict between the left and the right in our political decision making. There are many problems still to resolve. Having a clearer, less ambiguous, more widely accepted guideline will, nevertheless, be a major step forward to a more virtuous world.

REFERENCES

[1] Confucius, *Analects*, 1.1. This comes from the DC Lau translation. A different translation is used in chapter 2 note8 (p15).

[2] Cicero, *De senectute, On Old Age*, s2. The quotation also appears in chapter 5 (p33).

[3] Robert Burton, *The Anatomy of Melancholy*, using the text from a reprint of the sixth (1652) edition, by Chatto and Windus, London, 1883.

[4] Howard Harris, *Organizational Happiness*, in Oxford Research Encyclopedia of Business and Management.

CHAPTER 1. UNHAPPINESS IN OLDER PEOPLE

[1] Francisco Bagulho. (2002). Depression in Older People. *Current Opinions in Psychiatry*. 15(4).

[2] Andrew Dentino, et al. (1999.) Association of interleukin-6 and other biologic variables with depression in older people living in the community. *Journal of the American Geriatrics Society*,14(1), pp 6-11

[3] World Health Organization (2014). Preventing Suicide: A Global Imperative.

[4] www.beyondblue.org.au

[5] National Ageing Research Institute. (2009). Depression in older age: a scoping study. Final Report. Melbourne

[6] Available online, Black Dog Institute, www.blackdoginstitute.org.au.

CHAPTER 2. THE EARLY PHILOSOPHERS

[1] Plato's Counterfeit Sophists, Hakan Tell. Plato's philosophy was, in fact, almost immediately contested by Aristotle.

[2] Christopher Peterson (2008): *What Is Positive Psychology, and What Is It Not?* Available on the internet

[3] Olivia Rudgard (2017). Creativity linked 'to higher risk of suicide'. *Sydney Morning Herald*, March 18.

[4] Neel Burton. (2013). Aristotle on Happiness. Happiness is not a state but an activity. *Psychology Today*, Jan 28.

[5] Available on line. http://www.perseus.tufts.edu

[6] Oidinposha Imamkhodjaeva includes Jainism, and Mencius as Asian philosophies in his Oidinposha Imamkhodjaeva. Non-Violent Voices. *Philosophy Now.* Issue 124. 2018. Buddhism has adherents both ways.

[7] Confucius. (2010). *The Analacts, Book I,* London: Arcturus Publishing.

[8] Chris Fraser. (2013). Happiness in Classical Confucianism: Xunzi, *Philosophical Topics,* 41(1), pp. 53-79

[9] Readers can complete a simple happiness quiz on this blog, Google, "The Pursuit of Happiness", http://www.pursuit-of-happiness.org/

[10] Douglas Abrams. (ed.) (2016). *The Book of Joy: Lasting Happiness in a Changing World,* London: Hutchison.

CHAPTER 3. MARCUS TULLIUS CICERO

[1] The January–February 2012 issue of *Harvard Business Review,* although in the context of training Russian staff to smile at the newly opened McDonalds in Moscow

[2] W. D. Hooper (1917). Cicero's Religious Beliefs, *The Classical Journal,* 13(2), pp. 88-9

[3] These theories are now those of Immanuel Kant (four), Utilitarianism (also four), Virtue (six) and perhaps a half dozen combination theories.

[4] H. J. Haskell. (1964). *This was Cicero,* Greenwich: Fawcett Publications Inc. p. 296

CHAPTER 4. THE ANATOMY OF MELANCHOLY

[1] Eric Wilson. (2008). *Against Happiness: In Praise of Melancholy.* New York: Farrar, Straus and Giroux.

[2] Alain de Botton, (1997) *How Proust can save your life,* Picador. London

[3] See Francis Zimmerman, (1995) The History of Melancholy, *Journal of the International Institute.* 2(2).

[4] Mathew Del Nevo (2008). *The Valley Way of the Soul,* Sydney: St Pauls Publications.

[5] www.poets.org , search for Keats.

[6] Encyclopaedia Britannica on line
https://www.britannica.com/biography/Rene-Descartes

[7] Rudgard (2017). Creativity.

[8] The Public Domain Review, http://publicdomainreview.org/

[9] http://www.gutenberg.org/files

CHAPTER 5. MILL RUSSELL AND DARWIN

[1] John Stuart Mill. (1861) *Utilitarianism,* Available on line

[2] Daniel Goldman. (2016). *A Force for Good,* Bloomsbury publishing.

[3] Bjorn Grinde (2002). *Darwinian Happiness. Evolution as a Guide for Living and Understanding Human Behaviour.* London: The Darwin Press.

[4] Peter Crabb. (2003). Book Review Stalking the Good Life, *Evolutionary Psychology*, 1(1).

[5] Frederick Burkhardt, (1986). *The Correspondence of Charles Darwin, Volume 2: 1837-1843*, London: Walden Books.

CHAPTER 6. THE MODERN RESEARCHERS

[1] George E. Vaillant. (2003) Aging Well: Surprising Guideposts to a Happier Life from the Landmark Harvard Study of Adult Development, Boston, MA: Little Brown and Company.

[2] https://scienceblog.com/ April 11 ,2017

[3] B.R. Levy (2003) Mind Matters: Cognitive and Physical Effects of Aging Self-Stereotypes. Journal of Gerontology, 58(4) pp. 203-211.

[4] Felicia A. Huppert and Timothy T. C. So (2013 [2011]). Flourishing Across Europe: Application of a New Conceptual Framework for Defining Well-Being, Social Indicators Research, 110(3), pp. 837–861.

[5] Flinders University. The Australian Longitudinal Study of Ageing. Available on line

[6] The Organisation for Economic Co-Operation and Development (2001). The Well-being of Nations. The Role of Human and Social Capital. Brookings Inst Press.

[7] Paris: OECD Publishing. Available on line

[8] Ibid. Also available online

[9] James William (1902). Pragmatism and Other Writings. Penguin

[10] Richard Layard (2005) Happiness: Lessons from a New Science, London: Allen Lane

[11] Paul Martin (2014) Making Happy People: The nature of happiness and its origins in childhood, Harper Collins.

[12] In De Republica (The Republic, 51 B.C.) and De Legibus (On the Laws, 52 B.C).

[13] Available online under the title William Davies (2005). A Review of 'Happiness: Lessons from a New Science, by Richard Layard'.

[14] E. Diener et al. (2010). New well-being measures. Scales to assess flourishing and positive and negative feelings, Social Indicators Research, 97, pp. 143-156. and E. Diener (2009). Well-being for public policy, Oxford University Press. and D. Kahneman et al. (1999) Well-being: Foundations of hedonic psychology. Russell Sage Foundation.

CHAPTER 7. THE FINDINGS OF THE SURVEY

[1] Singer Renata (2015) *Older and Bolder Life After 60*, Melbourne University Publishing

[2] Le Figaro Damien. Mascret. Mis à jour le 09/03/2018.

[3] Gilles Berrut (2018). *Les papys qui font boom*. Paris : Solar Editions

CHAPTER 8. RELIGION, A HEALTHY LIFE, AND DEATH

[1] Hughes M. Helm et al. (2000). Does private religious activity prolong survival?, *Journal of Gerontology*, 55(7), pp.400–405.

[2] Robert A. Hummer et al. (1999). Religious involvement and U.S. adult mortality. *Demography*. 36(2), pp 273–285

[3] Institute for Natural Healing, (2016). *Harvard Study: Going to Church Boosts Health*, May 29, 2016. Available on line.

[4] Harold G. Koenig et al. (1999). Does Religious Attendance Prolong Survival? A Six-Year Follow-Up Study of 3,968 Older Adults. *Journal of Gerontology*. 54(7) pp. 370-376

[5] H. G. Koenig et al. (2001). *Handbook of Religion and Health*. New York: Oxford University Press.

[6] Pew Research Centre, (2010). *Tolerance and Tension: Islam and Christianity in Sub-Saharan Africa*, 15 April.

[7] E. Brooks Holifield (2014). Understanding Why Americans Seem More Religious Than Other Western Powers. *Huffington Post*. 15 February.

[8] Andrew Fenelon et al. (2016). Major Causes of Injury Death and the Life Expectancy Gap Between the United States and Other High-Income Countries, *Journal of the American Medical Association*, 315(6), pp. 609-611.

[9] Blaise Pascal (1623-1662) *Pensees*. Available free on line

[10] "Young people are leaving the faith" Our Sunday Visitor. https://www.osv.com/ Accessed 4 November, 2017

[11] Donald Paterson et al. (2007) *Ageing and physical activity: evidence to develop exercise recommendations for older adults*, Canadian Centre for Activity and Aging, University of Western Ontario.

[12] Mindful Nation UK (2015). *Report by the Mindfulness All-Party Parliamentary Group*. October, Available on line.

[13] Jackie Dent (2017). Is mindfulness all it's cracked up to be? *Sydney Morning Herald*, 7 April.

[14] On his website, http://www.milesneale.com/

[15] Harvard Medical School (2016). *How Mindfulness can change your brain and improve your health*.

[16] Thomas Zanzig and Marilyn Kielbasa (1996). *Christian Meditation for Beginners*. Minnesota: St Marys Press.

[17] Harvard Medical School (June, 2008) *Pets and your health*. Available on line.

[18] W. P. Anderson, C. M. Reid & G. L. Jennings (1992). *Pet ownership and risk factors for cardiovascular disease*. 157(5) pp. 298-301.

[19] University of York website, *'Dog-Speak' important for social bonding between pet and owner* 6 March 2018. Also published in Journal of Animal Cognition. 2 March, 2018

[20] pets site: psychologytoday.com

REFERENCES   115

[21] Cicero (45B [2012]). *Tusculan Disputations*, Gutenberg Press, Available on line.

[22] Letters of Epicurus to Idomeneus, Available online

[23] Internet Encyclopedia of Philosophy, Rene Descartes

[24] René Descartes [1641]. *Meditations on First Philosophy* (subtitled in which the existence of God and the immortality of the soul are demonstrated) (in Latin)

CHAPTER 9. THE ROLE OF GOVERNMENT

[1] Fred Miller (2012). Aristotle's Political Theory, The Stanford Encyclopedia of Philosophy (Fall 2012 Edition), Edward N. Zalta (ed.), URL = <https://plato.stanford.edu/archives/fall2012/entries/aristotle-politics/>.

[2] Paul Whitely and Harold D. Clarke (2016). Brexit: Why did older voters choose to Leave the EU. *The Independent*. 26 June.

[3] Lisa Cox (2014). Poll shows growing support for same-sex marriage. *Sydney Morning Herald*, 15 July.

[4] *The Guardian*, 19 June 2013

[5] UVA Center for Politics. (2017). *Center for Politics takes temperature of Trump voters at 100-day mark*. 27 April.

[6] Guillaume Tabard. (2017). Qui sont Les Francais qui votent pour Francois Fillon?. *Le Figaro*. 20 April.

[7] The All Party Parliamentary Group (United Kingdom) on Social Integration *Ages apart. Ties and divides across the generations*. December 04, 2017.

[8] Matthew Smith (2017). The "extremists" on both sides of the Brexit debate, *YouGov*, 1 August.

[9] Original polling commissioned by The Challenge and conducted by YouGov on behalf of the APPG on Social Integration. Available on: www.socialintegrationappg.org.uk

[10] Ibid

[11] Tax-free super is intergenerational theft: https://theconversation.com/

[12] https://www.yourlifechoices.com.au

CHAPTER 10. BRINGING IT TOGETHER

[1] In David Hume (1738). *Treatise of Human Nature*. Oxford University Press.

[2] Laelius de Amicitia ("Laelius on Friendship")

[3] Oxfam Davos report Published: 18 January 2016

[4] Larry Elliott (2017). World's eight richest people have same wealth as poorest 50%. *The Guardian*. 16 January.

[5] See Nancy Birdsall et al. (1993). *The East Asian miracle: economic growth and public policy: Main report (English)*. A World Bank policy research report. New York: Oxford University Press. http://documents.worldbank.org/curated/en/975081468244550798/Main-report

AFTERWORD

[1] James Fieser (1998). Hume's Wide Construal of the Virtues. *Modern Philosophy.* Twentieth World Congress of Philosophy: Boston, Massachusetts from August 10-15.

[2] Julia Annas. (2011). *Intelligent Virtue,* Oxford University Press.

[3] Neil Levy (2004). *What Makes us Moral.* Oxford: Oneworld Publications.

[4] Richard Joyce (2007). *The Evolution of Morality.* Cambridge, MA: MIT Press.

[5] Anthony J. Parel (2016). *Pax Gandhiana: The political philosophy of Mahatma Gandhi.* New York: Oxford University Press.

[6] Bertand Russell (1946). *Philosophy for the Layman.* Available on line: http://www.users.drew.edu/~jlenz/br-lay-philosophy.html

[7] Hugh Breakey (2012). 'Moral Pluralism' in Bowden P. (ed.). *Applied Ethics,* Melbourne: Tilde University Press

[8] Michael B. Gill and Shaun Nichols (2008). Sentimentalist Pluralism: Moral Psychology and Philosophical Ethics. *Philosophical Issues,* 18(1) pp. 143-163.

[9] J. Gibbs (2010). *Moral Development and Reality: Beyond the Theories of Kohlberg and Hoffman,* 2nd edn., Boston: Penguin Academics.

[10] Amy Coplan and Peter Goldie (2014). *Empathy: Philosophical and Psychological Perspectives.* Oxford University Press. and Melanie Killen and Judith Smetana (2014). *Handbook of Moral Development.* New York: Psychology Press.

[11] See "The Trolley Problem" on the web

[12] Leonardo Bursztyn et al. (2015). Moral Incentives: Experimental Evidence from Repayments of an Islamic Credit Card, *World Bank Policy Research Working Paper,* 7420

[13] Robert Nozick (1974). *Anarchy, State, and Utopia.* New York: Basic Books.

[14] Sunday Review (2017). *News Analysis: Syria Changed the World.* 17 April.

INDEX

A

Abraham Maslow, 41
Adam Smith, 96
Afterword, xiv
Ahimsa, 101
Alasdair MacIntyre, 93
al-Ghazālī, 102
Andrew Dentino, 1
Archbishop Desmond Tutu,, 17
Aristotle, xii, 8
Average age of YES and NO responders, 55

B

Barbara Fredrickson, 46
Beauchamp and Childress, 95
Beauchamp and Childress's, 95
Bernard Gert, 99
Beyond Blue, 2
Black Dog Institute, 2
Buddha, 15
Buddhism, 15

C

Character Strengths & Virtues, 42
Christopher Peterson, 41
Cicero, xii
Cicero,, 19
Confucius, 14
Corey Keyes, 43
Croesus, 6
Curiosity, 85

D

Dalai Lama, 15
David Hume, 87
De Legibus, 20
De Re Publica, 20
De Senectute, 22
Democritus Junior, 29
depression, xi

E

Ed Diener, 45
eudaimonia, 5
Euthanasia, 95

F

fading memory,, 1
Felicia Huppert, 39
Flinders University Centre for Ageing Studies, 39
Flourishing across Europe,, 39

G

George Washington,, 19
Geriatric Depression Test, 3
Greece, xiii
gun control, 95

H

happiness, xii
Harvard aging study, 37
Herodotus, xii, 5
Hippocrates, 5, 25

I

Immanuel Kant, 95
Islam, 102

J

John Adams,, 19
John F. Kennedy, 37
John Stuart Mill, 95
Jonathan Haidt, 43

M

Mahatma Gandhi's, 101
Marcel Proust, 26
Mark Antony,, 19
Martin Seligman, 40, 41
Mathew Del Nevo, 27
Melancholy, 25
Mencius, 14
Mihaly Csikszentmihalyi, 43
moral philosophy, 97

N

Neel Burton,, 9
Nichomachean Ethics, 8
NO answers, 49

O

On Youth and Old Age, 12
Oxfam, 89
Oxford [Ohio] Ageing Study, 38

P

Paul Martin, 44
PERMA, 41
Philosopher kings, 8
Plato, xii, 7
Pope Pius XII, 15
Positive psychology, 40
Principles of Psychology, 40
Probus, xiii

Q

Questionnaire, 50

R

Renata Singer, 57
response rate, 51
Richard Layard, 7, 44
Robert Burton., 28

S

same sex marriage, 95
Seneca the Younger, 25
Shakespeare, 19
Solon, xii
Stephen Pinker's, 96
stoicism, 21

T

The Anatomy of Melancholy, 28
the four noble truths, 16
The Republic, xiii, 6
Todd Kashdan, 44

U

United Nations, 40
University of the Third Age, xiii
US Declaration of
    Independence, 20

V

virtue, 93

W

website, xv
Well-being of Nations, 40
Widows, 57
William Frankena's, 98
William James, 40

X

Xenophon, 13

Z

Zeno of Cetium,, 26